PRESENTED TO:

....

FROM:

....

DATE:

....

THE
Nehemiah
CODE

It's Never Too Late
for a New Beginning

O. S. Hawkins

COUNTRYMAN ®

A Division of Thomas Nelson Publishers

THOMAS NELSON

Since 1798

Published in Nashville, Tennessee, by Thomas Nelson. Thomas Nelson is a registered trademark of HarperCollins Christian Publishing, Inc.

Thomas Nelson titles may be purchased in bulk for educational, business, fund-raising, or sales promotional use. For information, please e-mail SpecialMarkets@ThomasNelson.com.

ISBN: 978-0-7180-9138-5

Printed in China

18 19 20 21 22 DSC 6 5 4 3 2 1

I love the words of Nehemiah 1:11, which say,

"For I was the king's cupbearer."

The Nehemiah Code is dedicated to all those faithful "cupbearers" of King Jesus, faithful servants who ministered with dedication and determination in out-of-the-way, small places where they often wondered if they had been forgotten. They existed on meager pastors' salaries with little to nothing extra to put aside for their declining years. Since all the royalties and author's proceeds from *The Nehemiah Code* go to support them, you have a part in being Christ's hand extended to them by purchasing this book. Through Mission:Dignity, we are on a mission to bring dignity and security to retired pastors, their wives, and, now in most cases, their widows, helping them live out their final years without being financially forgotten. As one almost-ninety-year-old pastor's widow wrote recently, "Thanks to Mission:Dignity, I get to eat at night now, and it is not just a piece of toast." Learn more about Mission:Dignity by visiting www.GuideStone.org and clicking on "Mission:Dignity."

TABLE OF CONTENTS

INTRODUCTION
The Nehemiah Code

It's Never Too Late for a New Beginning

*R*ebuilding. Who among us is not in need of an occasional new beginning as we journey through different periods of life? Some of us deal with relationships that need to be rebuilt. Some are in the process of rebuilding businesses. Most coaches are continually engaged in the rebuilding process. Other people are seeking to rebuild their integrity after a misstep. Some are seeking to rebuild after divorce. Many who have lost loved ones are rebuilding their own lives. Some are rebuilding self-confidence and hoping for a better future. In one way or another, most of us will spend some or much of the next year trying to rebuild something. The good news is . . . *it's never too late for a new beginning.*

Nehemiah lived twenty-five hundred years ago, and he "wrote the book" on rebuilding. God recorded it for us and placed it in the Bible for all posterity. Who was Nehemiah (pronounced Nee-uh-mí-uh)? He was neither a preacher nor a prophet. Nehemiah was a civil servant, an ordinary guy, who applied some universal principles that enabled him to rebuild a broken city and, in the process, a lot of broken hopes. He has left us some secrets to his success, a sort of hidden "code" if you will, which can become a fountain of hope and strength to anyone and everyone who will apply his formula. The journey we are about to make, as we walk with him through the pages of his book, will enable us to apply some marvelous truths to our lives and to step into a new beginning ourselves.

Nehemiah's story unfolds after the reign of King Solomon in Jerusalem. The kingdom was now divided. The Northern Kingdom of Israel had been ruled by a series of wicked kings, not a good one among them. Then, in 722 BC, the Assyrian assault swept them away into a captivity from which they never returned. The Southern Kingdom lasted until 586 BC, when it was finally devastated and destroyed by the Babylonians. Their holy city of Jerusalem was virtually leveled and decimated. The temple was demolished, the wall of the city was broken down, and its gates were burned. The leading Jews were taken away as captives to Babylon, and once there, the psalmist says they hung their harps upon the willow trees in deep despair (Psalm 137:1–2). After several years, the Persians broke the Babylonian supremacy and allowed some of the Jews to return home, which they did. They began to rebuild their temple and city, but the sheer magnitude of the task caused them to give up. Years passed. The city, still broken and burned, was in dire need of rebuilding.

In stepped Nehemiah, a Jew still in exile, with a cushy civil service job complete with benefits and retirement. But Jerusalem burned in his heart. He left Babylon to return to Jerusalem, armed with a single, focused objective to rally the people, rebuild their hope, and, ultimately, rebuild their Holy City.

Nehemiah had a plan for rebuilding. He saw the end from the beginning. He got started right, he built a team spirit with those around him, and he finished strong. In doing so, he provides us with a "code" in these following pages that, if applied to our own experience, can enable us to rebuild some broken walls in our own lives and reinforce our own legacies. Nehemiah's message to us across the centuries is plain and powerful: *It is never too late for a new beginning!*

The longest journey always begins with the first step, so let's turn the page and learn how to "get started right."

PART 1

Rebuilders

Get Started Right

*T*hose successful in rebuilding their lives or their legacies have one thing in common: they get started right. If you are a golfer, you are keenly aware that the most important shot in golf is the tee shot, the first shot. Every new hole presents the golfer with a new beginning. At each hole, you step up onto the tee and hit your first shot. That shot generally determines how well you will play the hole. If you drive the ball into the woods, you have to scramble with a second and often a third shot just to get on the green. If your tee shot goes out of bounds, you are penalized additional strokes and the loss of distance. However, if you drive the ball straight down the fairway and into position for the second shot to the green, you are well on your way to achieving your goal of par for the hole. So many players never score well in golf because they spend most of their time trying to make up yardage lost by poor tee shots. Getting a good start is essential, whether we are playing golf or seeking to rebuild a life.

There is a real sense in which *rebuilding* something is

often a bigger challenge than building something from scratch. During my days as a pastor, I was privileged to lead two of the greatest churches in America. Both were in the heart of a city, downtown, in the midst of millions of people. One was in a cosmopolitan, secular, and virtually unchurched area on the south Florida coast. The other was a historic congregation in Texas filled with tradition and deeply held heritage. The challenge in Florida was to build a myriad of ministries without a lot of history and tradition. The task in Texas was not to build, but to *rebuild* on the foundation laid by two previous pastors who had collectively served the church for an entire century. The effort at the second church was by far the more difficult.

When we are in the process of rebuilding (no matter what it is we are seeking to rebuild), there are not just things that need to be *done*, but things that need to be *undone* as well. There are habits that need to be broken and sometimes hearts that need to be healed. Anyone who has ever sought to rebuild a marriage, a business, a dream, or a church knows this to be true. It often is simply easier to walk away and start over than it is to invest the effort and energy needed for rebuilding. If we are ever going to be successful in rebuilding, it is essential that we get started right.

For some, simply getting started—much less getting started right—is the hardest part of the entire rebuilding process. Fortunately for us, Nehemiah was an expert on getting started right. For decades, the Jews had seen the need to rebuild the broken wall and burned gates of Jerusalem. Some had even given it a try, then faltered and failed because of the sheer volume of the task. Nehemiah, however, came on the scene and accomplished this awesome task in less than two months. And a huge factor in his success was in the way he got started. In the first chapter of the Bible book bearing his name, Nehemiah's example outlines for us four steps to getting started in our own rebuilding process. Rebuilders get started right by

1. making an honest evaluation,
2. identifying with the need,
3. taking personal responsibility, and
4. moving out of their comfort zones.

These principles work no matter what we are seeking to rebuild in life. Consider it this way: Have you ever needed to lose some weight? I have. Have you ever needed to start an exercise program? I have. Have you ever needed to rebuild a broken relationship that is lying dormant? I have. And we both know that the hardest part of any of those challenges is just getting started. Nehemiah devoted the first chapter of his book to getting started with the rebuilding task. The rest of his book then relates to the unfolding principles that, when applied, will enable us to accomplish our own personal rebuilding tasks.

So now it is time to step up to the first tee, tee up your ball, and hit it straight down the middle of the fairway. Yes, rebuilders get started right, and when they do, they discover . . . *it's never too late for a new beginning!*

1   MAKE AN HONEST EVALUATION

The words of Nehemiah the son of Hachaliah. It came to pass in the month of Chislev, in the twentieth year, as I was in Shushan the citadel, that Hanani one of my brethren came with men from Judah; and I asked them concerning the Jews who had escaped, who had survived the captivity, and concerning Jerusalem. And they said to me, "The survivors who are left from the captivity in the province are there in great distress and reproach. The wall of Jerusalem is also broken down, and its gates are burned with fire."

—NEHEMIAH 1:1–3

Nehemiah opened his memoirs with the news of a report he received from distant Jerusalem. Hearing of someone who had recently returned from a visit, Nehemiah inquired about the status of the Jewish people and the condition of the Holy City itself. The report was not what he had hoped to hear: "The survivors who are left from the captivity in the province are there in great distress and reproach. The wall of Jerusalem is also broken down, and its gates are burned with fire" (Nehemiah 1:3).

If Nehemiah was to get started right in his task of rebuilding, his first step was to *make an honest evaluation* of the condition of Jerusalem. Although a remnant of the Jews had returned to their homeland and the temple was in place, there was only a semblance of normalcy. The wall of the city was still broken down from the destruction years earlier when the Babylonians had devastated the city. The gates were still unhinged, burned with fire. Those who had returned had dishonored God with their lifestyles and neglect of the temple, and they found themselves mired in deep "distress."

It was time to face the facts. First, the broken wall was in need of being rebuilt to provide safety and security for the inhabitants of Jerusalem. And, second, as long as the gates were burned, the enemy would have easy access to the city.

Many of us falter and fail in the rebuilding process at this very point—we don't take the time to make a thorough and careful enough evaluation of our circumstances and situation. For some, it is hard to get to the place of admitting our need, of

> We will never get started right until we make our own honest evaluation of the situation.

admitting that some of our own walls are broken and some of our own gates are burned. I know men and women who have met premature death because they would not face the warning signs of pain in their bodies. We all know those who waited too long to go to a physician to get an honest evaluation of their situation. The same can often be said regarding relationships, or, for that matter, anything else that needs to be rebuilt. If we are ever going to rebuild, we must first get started right. And we will never get started right until we make our own honest evaluation of the situation.

There are at least three approaches people take when seeking to rebuild something that is broken in their lives. One is the way of the "superficial optimist." The emphasis here is on the word *superficial*. This is a cosmetic approach that deals only with surface issues. These are people who are constantly in the process of trying to put a positive spin on difficult situations, often pretending a problem does not even exist. The superficial optimist will resist making any semblance of an honest evaluation, wishfully thinking that if he or she just waits long enough or hunkers down deep enough then everything will eventually be made right. The ancient prophet Jeremiah had this person in mind when he said there were some who say, "'Peace, peace!' When there is no peace" (Jeremiah 8:11).

Then, there are others who approach the process of rebuilding as "busy optimists." That is, they admit there is a problem, but they attack it by trying to get everyone around them to be as busy as they can be. These people set up new structures and new organizational charts. They acquire new personnel. They develop new slogans and motivate the troops with all types of positive-thinking techniques. But they never get around to honestly evaluating and addressing the situation. And all the new policies, new people, new plans, and new procedures in the world can't keep a ship afloat if it has holes in the hull.

Finally, there are those like Nehemiah, who make an honest evaluation of the situation right from the beginning. They have the courage to face the root problems and deal with them directly. We might refer to them as "honest optimists." They have the strength and patience, as well as the wisdom and understanding, to address the systemic issues and actually work to correct them. Those who make such honest evaluations are not afraid of offending others or making enemies. They are not intimidated by threats, and they cannot be formed and fashioned into someone else's mold. Such a person is our man, Nehemiah. He got started right by making an honest evaluation of his situation.

There may be many reading these words who are

in need of rebuilding—perhaps it's a relationship, self-confidence, or even a life—but they have never arrived at the place of admitting it. Perhaps you take the superficial optimist's approach, simply dealing with surface issues and ever saying "'Peace, peace!' when there is no peace." Or it may be that you more closely identify with the busy optimist. Instead of honestly evaluating your situation, you busily cover up the problems by moving on to new people and new projects. Learn from Nehemiah, the "honest optimist." Look at him. Listen to him. He made an honest evaluation. He inquired. He learned. Then he admitted that, not only was the wall broken down and the gates burned off their hinges, but the people were in distress. And, as if that were not bad enough, they had become a reproach to their God.

Is there any unfinished business in your life? Are there any walls that need rebuilding? Those who win at the game of life always finish what they start. But, before that can happen, they get a good start by making an honest evaluation of the problem. Rebuilders who go through the painful process of accurately assessing their situations are soon on the road to the realization that . . . *it's never too late for a new beginning!*

2 IDENTIFY WITH THE NEED

So it was, when I heard these words, that I sat down and wept,
and mourned for many days; I was fasting and praying before
the God of heaven.

—NEHEMIAH 1:4

*W*hen Nehemiah heard the report from Jerusalem
and made an honest evaluation of its broken wall
and burned gates, his passion index rose. His immediate impulse was to identify with the need. He wept. He
mourned. He fasted and prayed for days (Nehemiah 1:4).
This was not some faraway problem for Nehemiah; this
was personal.

Notice, too, that he "sat down." He didn't rush into
his task. He put everything else aside and contemplated
the matter. And as he did, he "wept." As he thought about
the reproach and the distress of the people of Jerusalem, a
lump rose in his throat and tears welled up in his eyes and
ran down his cheeks. The more I have studied the process
of rebuilding, the more convinced I have become that one
never rebuilds until he personally identifies with the need

and weeps over the ruins. We live in a culture that seems to have lost its tears. Much of contemporary Western Christianity focuses primarily on personal enjoyment. We seldom hear of the type of passion and vulnerability Nehemiah showed here.

Nehemiah's first concern in becoming the agent of rebuilding was not the welfare of the people, but the glory of his God. For him, prayer was warfare. He agonized. He wept. He mourned for days. He fasted. Is it any wonder he became God's chosen man to instigate and initiate the rebuilding of God's own Holy City? Nehemiah did what all godly leaders must do: he drew strength from outside himself, from his Lord. He identified with those in need, and he lived daily with this burden for four months.

> Nehemiah's first concern in becoming the agent of rebuilding was not the welfare of the people, but the glory of his God.

What about your passion index? Because without a passion for your rebuilding "project," you will, most likely, never see your goal accomplished. It is not enough to be honest about your need, if you do not identify with it passionately. In fact, without this brokenness and passion, the whole process of rebuilding will be just another burden layered on top of your already broken dreams. Those who get on with the actual process of rebuilding are the ones who passionately identify with the needs of the situation. Sadly, there are many who are simply not grieved or burdened about the walls in their lives that are broken and in need of rebuilding. It has been far too long since some of us have "sat down," much less "wept, and mourned for many days."

Take a marriage in need of rebuilding, for example. To be restored it takes a repentant heart on the part of the offending party and a receptive heart on the part of the offended party. I have known couples during my pastoral years who never rebuilt their relationships because of this very fact—they simply never could bring themselves to take responsibility to properly evaluate their situation and identify with the need themselves. It was always entirely the other person's fault.

Rebuilders get started right. And they know the only way to do this is to make an honest evaluation, which then leads to a personal identification with the need and with those around them. In the next step, we will see that Nehemiah also brought his people a true sense of camaraderie. He was, by his own example of leadership, letting everyone know . . . *it's never too late for a new beginning!*

3 TAKE PERSONAL RESPONSIBILITY

*And I said: "I pray, L*ORD *God of heaven, O great and awesome God, You who keep Your covenant and mercy with those who love You and observe Your commandments, please let Your ear be attentive and Your eyes open, that You may hear the prayer of Your servant which I pray before You now, day and night, for the children of Israel Your servants, and confess the sins of the children of Israel which we have sinned against You. Both my father's house and I have sinned. We have acted very corruptly against You, and have not kept the commandments, the statutes, nor the ordinances which You commanded Your servant Moses. Remember, I pray, the word that You commanded Your servant Moses, saying, 'If you are unfaithful, I will scatter you among the nations; but if you return to Me, and keep My commandments and do them, though some of you were cast out to the farthest part of the heavens, yet I will gather them from there, and bring them to the place which I have chosen as a dwelling for My name.' Now these are Your servants and Your people, whom You have redeemed by Your great power, and by Your strong hand. O Lord, I pray, please let Your ear be attentive to the prayer of Your servant, and to the prayer of Your servants who*

desire to fear Your name; and let Your servant prosper this day,
I pray, and grant him mercy in the sight of this man."

For I was the king's cupbearer.

—NEHEMIAH 1:5–11

*N*ehemiah could have approached the process of rebuilding Jerusalem by pointing the finger of accusation at those who bore responsibility for the current dilemma. If Nebuchadnezzar had not besieged Jerusalem, burned it, and taken the captives into Babylon, the Jews would not have had this huge task of rebuilding before them. Perhaps if Zerubbabel had been a bit more zealous about the task of rebuilding years earlier, when the remnant began to return from exile, things would have been different. Nehemiah had a lot of people—with their past mistakes and difficulties—he could have blamed for all the current problems. He could have rightly placed blame on Jehoiachin, Zedekiah, and the other kings of Judah. They had betrayed their people and their heritage by turning away from their God, resulting in the devastation of their people, their temple, and their city. But Nehemiah was wise enough to know that those who play the blame game never get the task of rebuilding completed. He refused to direct the blame to others and, instead, stepped up to take personal responsibility himself.

Too many people fall into the trap of blaming their present problems on the wrong decisions made by other people in the past. But falling into this trap never leads to moving forward with actually accomplishing our own tasks. Nehemiah ultimately had one goal: getting the wall rebuilt. And he was laser-focused on getting this task started right.

Listen to Nehemiah's plea as he confessed to God the sins of the people of Israel: "We have sinned against You. Both my father's house and I have sinned. We have acted very corruptly against You" (Nehemiah 1:6–7). Note the plural pronoun "we." For Nehemiah, it was "we," not "they." True rebuilders identify with the fears and failures of those around them. They take personal responsibility for the situation—even if the problems didn't begin with them. Do you see how Nehemiah was team building early on in this process? He confessed other people's sins as if they were his own. There was no "*You* made a mistake." There was no "*You* have sinned . . ." Instead, Nehemiah cried out to God with two key and personal words: "we" and "I."

> True rebuilders identify with the fears and failures of those around them.

Taking personal responsibility is the very point that

keeps some from getting started on the process of rebuilding. They prefer for someone else to be blamed for the condition of their own broken walls and burned gates. It always has to be someone else's fault. This is why so many homes stay broken and so many relationships are burned. It never dawns on some of us that we should take personal responsibility. We are too busy with the task of making excuses and justifying ourselves. But the fact is that the task of rebuilding will never be accomplished until and unless we take personal responsibility.

It only takes one person to get the entire process of rebuilding started, whether it is in a relationship, in the home, or at the office. Nehemiah decided to become that person. And he left a lasting legacy testifying to the fact that one person, who is willing to take the initiative, can make a huge difference and be living proof that . . . *it's never too late for a new beginning!*

4 MOVE OUT OF YOUR COMFORT ZONE

O Lord, I pray, please let Your ear be attentive to the prayer of Your servant, and to the prayer of Your servants who desire to fear Your name; and let Your servant prosper this day, I pray, and grant him mercy in the sight of this man.

For I was the king's cupbearer.

—NEHEMIAH 1:11

Comfort zones. We all have them. Those areas of life from which we seldom, if ever, like to venture. For some, there are racial comfort zones. In these people's lives, little interaction ever takes place with anyone outside their own skin color or ethnic background. Others live in economic comfort zones. That is, they find their fellowship primarily with those in their own socioeconomic circles and seldom venture far outside them. Some live in political comfort zones. They don't have much to do with those who don't think as they do or vote for the same people and parties they promote. If we are honest, we'll admit that, more often than not, comfort zones present one of the biggest obstacles to rebuilding.

Nehemiah concluded the first chapter of his book with a final and seemingly benign sentence, "For I was the king's cupbearer" (Nehemiah 1:11). On the surface it certainly does not sound too impressive. What was he? A dishwasher? A waiter? Or was he some type of a busboy? This statement seems so out of context with the rest of the chapter; it just hangs there like some sort of dangling addendum. But there is so much behind this simple sentence. Nehemiah was, in fact, the king's most trusted confidant. He was constantly by the king's side. He tasted every drop of drink and every morsel of food before it went into the king's mouth. Nehemiah was no busboy; he was the faithful counsel to the most important man in the land.

The fact that Nehemiah had risen up through the ranks to become the "king's cupbearer" speaks volumes about his own character and reputation. Persia was the world power of its day, and the king would select only the wisest, most honest, most loyal and trustworthy person he could find to be his personal cupbearer. The point Nehemiah is making with this statement is simply this—he had made it. He was fixed for life. He had a civil service job with what must have been incredible benefits. Yet he was willing to

Must be led by god

move out of his own comfort zone in order to be the agent of rebuilding in Jerusalem.

One of the reasons there is so little rebuilding of relationships and lives today is that too few of us are willing to step out of our own self-imposed comfort zones. We like our "benefits," and we aren't particularly willing to sacrifice them—not to help another and not to bring glory to God.

> One of the reasons there is so little rebuilding of relationships and lives today is that too few of us are willing to step out of our own self-imposed comfort zones.

I am a Texas boy, born and bred, and like all the rest of us, I'm pretty proud of it. Most boys growing up in Texas live for the fall and football season. The one common characteristic of all the great professional football teams in the modern era is that their dynasty was built around one person who was proficient at throwing the football. Look at the Green Bay Packers from Bart Starr to Aaron Rodgers, the Dallas Cowboys from Roger Staubach to Tony Romo, the Baltimore and Indianapolis Colts from Johnny Unitas to Peyton Manning. Throwing the forward pass in football is risky business. Darrell Royal, the late, legendary coach at the University of Texas, said four things happen when you throw the forward pass, and three of them are bad. You can complete the pass, and that is good. But the bad things are that the quarterback can get tackled for a loss; the pass can fall to the ground incomplete, resulting in a wasted down; or, worse yet, the pass can get intercepted by the other team.

There was a time when football teams lived within a different comfort zone. The year was 1905. The games were low scoring and fought down in the trenches with running, tackling, and kicking. Guys wearing only leather helmets flung their bodies through the air, running and blocking in a "flying wedge." It was three hard yards and a cloud of dust. It was a tough, dirty, gritty game played "between the tackles." But then something happened in 1906. The forward pass was legalized, making it possible to gain as much as forty yards with the flick of a wrist. During that first season, however, few teams utilized it. They stayed within their comfort zones. They kept running, over and over and over. They kept doing what they had always done. It was comfortable. Then, realizing a new day had come, St. Louis University became one of the first to move out of its comfort zone. They switched almost entirely to the forward pass, and that first season they outscored their opponents 402–11. The rest is football history.

Rebuilding means that, at times, we have to move out of our own comfort zones. This is exactly what Jesus did when He laid aside His glory in heaven, encased Himself in human flesh, and walked among us. And He is still constantly calling on men and women to leave their comfort zones and follow after Him.

Listen again to Nehemiah: "For I was the king's cupbearer." "So what?" you may ask. "Why does that matter?" It matters because of all that is behind those six words. It meant leaving his comfort zone. It meant taking a risk. It meant returning to Jerusalem. It meant becoming vulnerable. But the end result would be rewarding. Nehemiah would go on to become the agent of an incredible rebuilding process that would bring much good to others and much glory to his God.

Are there walls in your life in need of repair? Are there burned gates that are leaving you exposed and vulnerable? Be honest. Perhaps your wall isn't completely broken down, but a stone is missing here or there, and little cracks are appearing. Remember, the Lord Jesus left His own comfort zone of heaven to become the rebuilder of our broken walls. Through the pen of Isaiah, His prophet, He said, "Can a woman forget her nursing child, and not have compassion on the son of her womb? Surely they may forget, yet I will not forget you. See, I have inscribed you on the palms of My Hands, your walls are continually before Me" (Isaiah 49:15–16). Our Lord saw that our walls of life were in need of rebuilding. What did He do about it? He came to be our personal rebuilder. And He got started right. He made an honest evaluation, and then He identified with our need. He, like Nehemiah, came and wept over us and over the city of Jerusalem. Next, He took personal responsibility. He took our sin into His own body and died our death so that we could live His life; taking our sin so we could take His righteousness. He came to be the rebuilder of the broken walls of your life.

Go ahead, get up, and move out of your comfort zone. When you do, you will be getting started right, and you will be on your way to discovering the truth that . . . *it's never too late for a new beginning!*

PART 2

Rebuilders

Build a Team Spirit

$\mathscr{N}$ehemiah is proving to be a wise sage when it comes to the process of rebuilding. Now, as we continue on our journey with Nehemiah, we come to the second important lesson in rebuilding: rebuilders build a team spirit. They do away with the perpendicular pronoun "I," and they choose instead to say "we" . . . a lot. This truth is woven throughout the fabric of the second chapter of Nehemiah's memoirs as we watch him build a team spirit with those around him. The ability to work together and not against one another is an essential element of rebuilding. This is true whether we are seeking to rebuild a life, a business, a church, an athletic team, a marriage, self-confidence, or whatever. The simple fact is this: rebuilding is a team sport.

The most successful athletic franchises are those whose players do not care who gets the headlines or the credit; they operate as one unified body. Take, for example, the year 1998. It was one of the most memorable seasons in Major League Baseball. Throughout most of that summer, the spotlight beamed down on two individuals on center stage: Mark McGwire and Sammy Sosa. They were involved in a nail-biting home run race that eventually saw McGwire break the all-time home run record for a single season. (Subsequently, in 2010, he admitted to using strength-enhancing drugs during that 1998 season. Sosa tested positive during the 2003 season.) Though these two superstars remained in the center of attention, neither of their teams made it to the World Series. Instead, it was the New York Yankees who set a record for most wins in a season and won the big prize that year. And the Yankees did it without one major superstar rising above the others on the team. They played as a team. It was one for all and all for one, and they won it all.

Teamwork isn't just for the athletic field either. Experience also reveals that the most successful homes are built by families who play together as a team. The most successful businesses are those in which every employee is valued, and they all work together as a team. Getting started right may be essential, but building a team spirit is what adds fuel to the rebuilding process and keeps it moving toward a successful completion.

Nehemiah was a master at building a team spirit, and he utilized five principles to accomplish his task—principles that we can incorporate into our own rebuilding projects.

First, we must start with our goal in mind. People want to know where we are leading them and how we intend to get them there. Before he ever left Persia for Jerusalem, before he recruited his first fellow worker, before he motivated his people, Nehemiah started with his goal of rebuilding the broken wall in mind. Next, we must seize our opportunities. Listen to Nehemiah as he pleaded with the king to "send me" to Jerusalem (Nehemiah 2:5). These are the words of a man who passionately seized the opportunity before him and would not let it go. Third, we must make a careful analysis of our situation. That is, like Nehemiah, we must take a close, careful, and honest look at the ruins that need to be rebuilt in our own lives. For the fourth step, we must motivate our people to get off dead center. And then for the final step in building a team spirit, Nehemiah speaks of the importance of staying on track. If our own process of rebuilding is to be completed, we must work on it as a team without letting anyone or anything divert us or get us off track.

Rebuilders keep focused. They build a team spirit because they are smart enough to know they cannot do it all on their own. And they are also convinced that . . . *it's never too late for a new beginning!*

START WITH YOUR GOAL IN MIND

And it came to pass in the month of Nisan, in the twentieth year of King Artaxerxes, when wine was before him, that I took the wine and gave it to the king. Now I had never been sad in his presence before. Therefore the king said to me, "Why is your face sad, since you are not sick? This is nothing but sorrow of heart."

So I became dreadfully afraid, and said to the king, "May the king live forever! Why should my face not be sad, when the city, the place of my fathers' tombs, lies waste, and its gates are burned with fire?"

—NEHEMIAH 2:1–3

efore Nehemiah ever left Persia, before he ever recruited his first coworker, before he ever placed the first stone in the wall of Jerusalem, he lived with a burden and started with his goal in mind. He knew where he was going. He knew how he was going to get there. And he knew what he was going to do.

Nehemiah's boss, the king, noticed something was

troubling him and asked, "Why is your face sad since you are not sick? This is nothing but sorrow of heart" (Nehemiah 2:2). For four long months, Nehemiah had been living with this burden, ever since he first heard the exile's report of the broken wall and burned gates of the city of Jerusalem. So his reply to the king's question is a frank illustration of the fact that his goal was in his mind long before he ever left Persia for Jerusalem: "Why should my face not be sad, when the city, the place of my fathers' tombs, lies waste, and its gates are burned with fire?" (2:3). Nehemiah had a passion for what God had planted in his heart: to rebuild Jerusalem! His heart was laid bare upon his face, and his king read him like a book. Here is a man who was living with his goal in mind and on his heart.

Anyone who has ever been successful in the process of rebuilding in life knows where he is going and how he plans on getting there. In our sports-crazed Western world, there are a few faces who are globally recognized and revered. One is that of Michael Jordan, arguably the greatest basketball player to ever step on a court. Words are useless to attempt to describe his athletic prowess. For fifteen years he dominated the NBA as he played for the Chicago Bulls. During that entire time span, he averaged a remarkable thirty-two points a game. No matter who the Bulls were playing, where they were playing, who was guarding him, or what injuries he may have been nursing, he managed to score thirty-two points on average each time he entered a game. A reporter once asked him how he was able to maintain this average over a career spanning so many years. Jordan replied, "I simplify the matter. It takes only eight points a quarter to average thirty-two points per game. I find some way each quarter to simply get those eight points, four baskets." What was Michael Jordan doing? The same thing Nehemiah did, and the same thing any of us who are rebuilders do. He started each game with a goal in mind. He knew what he needed to do and how he was going to get it done. Those of us in need of rebuilding could learn an important lesson from both Michael Jordan and Nehemiah. Starting with our goal in mind is essential to building a team spirit so that we may finish the work of rebuilding.

The goal Nehemiah had in mind is readily apparent when we read the second chapter of his book. In a few pages, we will see that he was joined by hundreds of people who would follow his leadership and, with tools in hand, rebuild the wall.

There are a lot of broken-down walls around a lot of homes today

> There are a lot of broken-down walls around a lot of homes today because men and women have no real goal in mind and little idea about where they are going.

because men and women have no real goal in mind and little idea about where they are going. But the fact is that these goals are clearly delineated for us in the New Testament book of Ephesians. The husband holds the key to the home by loving his wife selflessly and sacrificially just as Christ loves the church (5:25). It is easy for a family to respond in loving, mutual submission to that kind of love because it always has our highest interest in mind. When a husband loves as Christ does, his attitude builds a team spirit that is difficult, if not impossible, to resist or defeat.

The reason many businesses and churches—and lives for that matter—are stagnant or in a death spiral is because they have never built a team spirit. Why? Because they have no goal in mind. They do not know where they are going, much less how they are going to get there. Rebuilders know where they are headed. They know how they plan to get there. And they are keenly cognizant of the fact that . . . *it's never too late for a new beginning!*

6 SEIZE YOUR OPPORTUNITIES

Then the king said to me, "What do you request?"

So I prayed to the God of heaven. And I said to the king, "If it pleases the king, and if your servant has found favor in your sight, I ask that you send me to Judah, to the city of my fathers' tombs, that I may rebuild it."

Then the king said to me (the queen also sitting beside him), "How long will your journey be? And when will you return?" So it pleased the king to send me; and I set him a time.

Furthermore I said to the king, "If it pleases the king, let letters be given to me for the governors of the region beyond the river, that they must permit me to pass through till I come to Judah, and a letter to Asaph the keeper of the king's forest, that he must give me timber to make beams for the gates of the citadel which pertains to the temple, for the city wall, and for the house that I will occupy." And the king granted them to me according to the good hand of my God upon me.

Then I went to the governors in the region beyond the River, and gave them the king's letters. Now the king had sent captains of the army and horsemen with me. When Sanballat the Horonite and Tobiah the Ammonite official heard of it, they were deeply disturbed that a man had come to seek the well-being of the children of Israel.

—NEHEMIAH 2:4–10

*I*n the second chapter of his book, we find Nehemiah standing in the presence of King Artaxerxes. The king, acknowledging Nehemiah's sad countenance, made a pointed inquiry: "What do you request?" (Nehemiah 2:4). Immediately, Nehemiah seized his opportunity: "Send me to Judah, the city of my father's tombs, that I may rebuild it" (2:5). There was not an ounce of delay or doubt about him. He took advantage of this open door of opportunity and went straight to the point. Then, in rapid succession, the king asked more questions: "How long will your journey be? And when will you return?" (2:6). Nehemiah had been planning and waiting for this moment for months, and when it presented itself, Nehemiah was ready to seize it. He had thought it through and had already considered all the possible questions, so he had all the right answers ready for the king's inquiry. Successful rebuilders, whether they are rebuilding rubble or relationships, have a way of seizing opportunities when they come their way.

Many people never get started in the rebuilding process because they are always "waiting for God to open a door for them." In my own experience, I have found that opportunity doesn't usually come knocking at my door out of nowhere. More often than not, opportunity is found opening the door when I am the one doing the knocking! It is somewhat akin to what Knute Rockne, the revered Notre Dame football coach, once said about prayer, "I've found that prayers work best when you have big players." Opportunities most often come our way when we are knocking on the door and not simply waiting for an opportunity to knock.

> Many people never get started in the rebuilding process because they are always "waiting for God to open a door" for them.

One of my favorite movie scenes is from the film *Dead Poets Society*, which starred the late Robin Williams. He played the role of John Keating, a new English professor in an elite, upper-crust, all-boys preparatory school in the Northeast of which he was an alumnus. It was a prep school with a long history of academic excellence and generations of wealthy, blue-blood graduates who went on to the Harvards and Yales of the world. Wanting to turn English literature from a musty, boring experience, he sought to breathe life into it and impart a spirit of conquest into his young students. During one class, he marches the boys out of the room and down the hallway, until they come to a row of large, glass-fronted cases along the wall. The cases contained the pictures of former students, long gone from those hallowed halls and many long gone from life itself. "Peruse some of the faces from the past," he says. "You've walked past them many times. I don't think you've really looked at them." The photos were old and faded, cracked and bent. Across the years those young men, like their photos, had grown old and faded themselves. The faces in the glass cases stared back at the young charges. "They're not that different from you, are they? . . . They believe they're destined for great things, just like many of you." Then, the teacher lowers his voice to almost a whisper. "But if you listen real close, you can hear them whisper their legacy to you." The young students press closer to the glass cases. "Carpe diem," he says. The professor whispers again, "Seize the day, boys. Make your lives extraordinary."

No message is timelier for anyone who seeks to be a rebuilder. Either we seize the opportunities when they are before us, or we let them pass by, only to live with the sad regrets of what might have been. Perhaps John Greenleaf Whittier, the Quaker American poet of the nineteenth century, framed it best in his poem entitled "Maud Muller": "For all sad words of tongue or pen, the saddest are these: 'It might have been!'"

The New Testament is replete with the stories of men

and women who seized their opportunities. James and John were both commercial fishermen in business with their father at Zebedee and Sons on the northeastern shore of the Galilee—until, that is, Jesus Christ walked by one day as they were mending their nets, looked them squarely in the eyes, and called them to join His team. Opportunity came knocking "and immediately, they left their boat and their father, and followed Him" (Matthew 4:22).

Once, in Capernaum, four friends sought to get their sick friend into Jesus' presence, but could not get near Him due to the massive crowd that filled the house where He was. Still, they seized the opportunity before them, climbed up on the roof, cut a hole in it, and lowered their friend right down at the feet of Jesus. When Jesus saw their faith, He instructed the lame man to get up and walk. "Immediately he arose, took up the bed, and went out" (Mark 2:12).

Once, when Jesus was passing by a village, there was a woman in the crowd who had suffered from a physical infirmity for twelve years. She had been to all the best doctors but to no avail. As Jesus passed by, she seized her moment and knocked on the door of opportunity. She burst forth from the crowd, reached out, and "touched the border of His garment. And immediately [*there is that word again*] her flow of blood stopped" (Luke 8:44).

We are all what we are in life, in part, because of what we do when opportunities come our way. For many years, Nehemiah had been living in Persia. But all that time he had been living with Jerusalem in his heart . . . praying . . . planning . . . preparing. When opportunity came, he immediately seized it and made his request of the king—to be sent back to the land of Judah, back to Jerusalem, to be the rebuilder of its broken wall and burned gates.

Tragically, some of us never rebuild, even though we may have gotten started right. We failed to seize the opportunity when it came. It just might be that God is asking you today what the king asked Nehemiah: "What do you request?" Look at Nehemiah. Listen to him. Can you hear him? He is not whispering. He is shouting to us, "Carpe diem! Seize the day!" And if you listen closely enough, you will also hear him say . . . *it's never too late for a new beginning!*

7　MAKE A CAREFUL ANALYSIS OF YOUR SITUATION

So I came to Jerusalem and was there three days. Then I arose in the night, I and a few men with me; I told no one what my God had put in my heart to do at Jerusalem; nor was there any animal with me, except the one on which I rode. And I went out by night through the Valley Gate to the Serpent Well and the Refuse Gate, and viewed the walls of Jerusalem which were broken down and its gates which were burned with fire. Then I went on to the Fountain Gate and to the King's Pool, but there was no room for the animal under me to pass. So I went up in the night by the valley, and viewed the wall; then I turned back and entered by the Valley Gate, and so returned. And the officials did not know where I had gone or what I had done; I had not yet told the Jews, the priests, the nobles, the officials, or the others who did the work.

—NEHEMIAH 2:11–16

*B*efore the rebuilding process in Jerusalem had begun and before a single recruit had been enlisted for the challenging task, Nehemiah made a careful analysis of the situation before him. When he finally arrived in Jerusalem after a long journey of anticipation, he waited for three days before doing anything. Then, alone and in the middle of the night, he mounted a horse and surveyed the ruined walls in the moonlight shadows: "I told no one what my God had put in my heart to do at Jerusalem" (Nehemiah 2:12).

Leadership is often a lonely assignment. Before any major work of rebuilding is accomplished, someone must take his own midnight ride to honestly review the ruins of the situation. And often, as in the case of Nehemiah, that person must even weep over the ruins with deep compassion and determined concern. Note that Nehemiah did not send some underling to check out the situation and bring him back a written report with a suggested plan to go forward. There are some things that simply cannot be delegated in the process of rebuilding. It is part of the price of effective leadership. Those who lead others to accomplish great tasks in life usually struggle long and hard—and often alone—before their plans are ever made public. But one of the best ways leaders can build a team spirit among their own troops is to make sure they have all the facts right before they begin. Rebuilders do not rush into the process without doing their homework.

Nehemiah's nocturnal journey was not simply a perusal, a casual glance at the rubble and ruins. The Bible tells us that he "viewed" the broken-down walls (2:13–15). The Hebrew word we translate into our English Bibles as "viewed" is actually a medical term describing a physician who looks into a wound very carefully before taking any action. It describes a doctor who is probing a wound to fully assess its depth and damage. This was no casual glance.

My first pastorate was in the wheat-farming country of rural southwestern Oklahoma. On rare occasions, those old-timers would request that the pastor be in the operating room during their surgeries. With my city roots, I found this very strange, but it seemed to bring comfort to the few who asked me to do so. So, on those occasions I would "scrub up" with the local doctor and be present in the room to pray for the surgery. It was an amazing education for me. In high school biology classes, I had seen the diagrams of all the human organs, and they always appeared to be so neatly placed within our abdomens. Not so! I would watch that surgeon "probe" all the vital organs in an exploratory abdominal surgery. He would hold them up in his hands, examine them, and thoroughly "view" those organs that were so vital to a person's well-being. Then he would just stuff them—rather haphazardly, it seemed—back into the open abdominal cavity.

This kind of probing analysis is exactly the process Nehemiah used to describe what he did that evening when he took his midnight ride to "view" the wall of Jerusalem. This was no casual glimpse in the dark, but a careful sizing up of the situation. Nehemiah saw for himself all the broken debris that had been piling up for decades. There was accumulated trash all around the broken-down wall, and nothing had been done to remove it. This same accumulation of "trash" happens in so many lives today. I have seen it happen in marriages. I have seen it happen in business pursuits. I have even seen it happen in churches. Rubble has its own way of piling up over the years and getting in the way of healthy and wholesome relationships. And sadly, in too many cases, it is simply left there and nothing is done about it.

> Leadership is often a lonely assignment. Before any major work of rebuilding is accomplished, someone must take his own midnight ride to honestly review the ruins of the situation.

Successful rebuilders make their own careful and honest evaluation of the situation at hand. They also assess the debris—the bad attitudes and less-than-productive actions—that have been piling up across the years and that must be removed before the process of rebuilding can begin.

No matter how much debris is left lying around their walls, successful rebuilders make a careful analysis of their situation because they know . . . *it's never too late for a new beginning!*

8 MOTIVATE YOUR PEOPLE TO GET OFF DEAD CENTER

Then I said to them, "You see the distress that we are in, how Jerusalem lies waste, and its gates are burned with fire. Come and let us build the wall of Jerusalem, that we may no longer be a reproach." And I told them of the hand of my God which had been good upon me, and also of the king's words that he had spoken to me.

So they said, "Let us rise up and build." Then they set their hands to this good work.

—NEHEMIAH 2:17–18

*N*ehemiah was wise enough to know that before the actual process of rebuilding Jerusalem's burned gates and broken wall could begin, he first needed to build a team spirit among the workers by motivating them to action—to get off dead center, where they had been stuck for years.

Nehemiah was able to convince the people to adopt his vision because he followed three vital rules in goal setting. First, he made certain his goal of rebuilding was *conceivable*. That is, he made sure those around him could easily envision the plan of where they were going and how they were going to get there. Next, he made sure his goal of rebuilding was *believable*. These were goals his people could believe in. These men and women had been living in discouragement for years and needed to believe in something again. Hear his challenge: "Let's do it. We can get this done. The hand of our God is with us" (Nehemiah 2:17–18, author's paraphrase). The people not only conceived the goal, but they also began to believe it could be accomplished. Finally, Nehemiah made sure his goal was *achievable*. This goal was not outside their reach. They could do it. They could rebuild the broken wall. It was conceivable, believable, *and* it was achievable.

Nehemiah encouraged them: "You see the distress that we are in, how Jerusalem lies waste, and its gates are burned with fire. Come and let us build the wall of Jerusalem, that we may no longer be a reproach" (2:17). He reminded the people that God was with them—orchestrating, leading, and moving behind the scenes. And they got it. Listen to them rally to the task: "So they said, 'Let us rise up and build.' Then they set their hands to this good work" (2:18). Nehemiah then called on the people to adopt four attitudes that would result in getting off dead center. He led them to *face up*, *team up*, *gird up*, and *look up*.

Nehemiah began by having the people *face up.* "You see the distress that we are in, how Jerusalem lies waste, and its gates are burned with fire" (2:17). The people had been looking at the situation for a long time. But now he directs them to *see* it—to face up to it. They had become accustomed to looking daily at the city's broken wall. It no longer shocked them. It took someone coming from somewhere else to see it for what it really was: a dishonoring of God by allowing His Holy City to remain in such a state of ruin.

We will never rebuild our own broken walls until we, too, face up to the reality of our situation. This is true whether we are trying to rebuild a relationship, a marriage, a business, a church, a life, or whatever. It is ironic that it often takes someone with a fresh perspective to get us to face up and see things that exist right under our noses. Years of familiarity and neglect have a way of allowing us to *look* at certain things without really *seeing* them. This is why the wise counsel of a trusted friend is so valuable. We will never be motivated to complete our own task of rebuilding until we face up to the "distress" that looms around us.

> It is ironic that it often takes someone with a fresh perspective to get us to face up and see things that exist right under our noses.

Next, Nehemiah called on his people to *team up*. Note the repetition of the plural personal pronouns in his challenge: "we . . . us . . . we" (2:17). Nehemiah was smart enough to incorporate a lot of plural pronouns. He was subtly motivating his people to work *with* him and not *for* him. What type of response do you think he might have received if he had approached this the way some of us have done in the past? "You people are unbelievable. You have been here all these years and look at you. What have you been doing? You have gotten yourself into a pitiful and shameful situation. You know what you need to do, don't you? You need to get up and rebuild this broken wall. You are the reproach; not the wall. I am not the problem. I just got here. Now, get on with it." Note there is not a plural pronoun in the above statement. It is laced with "You . . . you . . . you . . . I . . . I . . . I."

Playing the blame game, coupled with constant criticism, will squelch motivation at every turn. By Nehemiah's repeated use of "I" and "we," he was saying, "Let's team up." How much better might our parenting have been had we said "we" more than "you"? How many marriages might have been saved if spouses had faced up and teamed up? How many pastors failed at rebuilding because they used their pulpits to berate and bully instead of using "we" a little more and building a team spirit? Rebuilders say "we" an awful lot. That's because they know rebuilding is a team sport.

Nehemiah also called on the people to *gird up*: "Come and let us rebuild the wall of Jerusalem" (Nehemiah 2:17). These people were not just following Nehemiah; they were following his vision. Needs are all around us. But in the long term, people do not give themselves to needs; they give themselves to visions. They want to be a part of something bigger than themselves. These people of Jerusalem had lived with the need to rebuild their broken wall for years and had done nothing about it. Then Nehemiah stepped in and gave them a vision of how to do it. This is one of the key components of the rebuilding process: no matter what we are trying to rebuild, we need a vision bigger than we are to accomplish the task.

Note that Nehemiah's approach was not an attempt to get the people to focus on the miserable state in which he found them upon his arrival. We don't motivate people to get off dead center by always trying to get them to look backward, but by getting them to look forward instead. Nehemiah challenged the people to do something tangible, to gird up and start putting one stone upon another. He had lived with this burden in his heart for months. He had wept on his lonely midnight ride surveying the wreckage. But he never tried to motivate the people out of guilt or sympathy. Instead, he used his optimism. It was his can-do spirit that inspired the people. I can hear this speech now: "We are going to do it. It is before us. Let's get up, gird up, and go for it. Let's do this together. We can do it!"

Then, finally, this master motivator called on the people to *look up*. He said, "I told them of the hand of my God which had been good upon me" (2:18). Nehemiah reminded the people that God was with them, and His hand was leading and guiding them to accomplish this task. Even today, people still have a way of rallying around something when they become convinced God is in it.

This is a good time to pause and ask ourselves a question: *What was Nehemiah's motive behind all this?* Was it to have the biggest wall in that part of the world? Was it so he could take center stage and show off his leadership finesse? Not in the least. His underlying motive is plainly revealed in Nehemiah 2:17: "That we may no longer be a reproach." His primary motive was for the glory of God, not himself.

No matter what needs rebuilding around our individual lives, the route to the final destination is the same for each of us. And these four motivating influences are essential:

- *Face up*: stop blaming others and deal with the real issue at hand.
- *Team up*: realize that we all need each other.

- *Gird up*: get off the couch, get out of bed, and begin to work on the issue at hand. Accept the fact that life goes on, and start placing one stone upon another.
- *Look up*: remember that it is never too late for a new beginning, no matter who you are or where you are.

When Nehemiah presented his challenge to the people of Jerusalem, their negative feelings began to turn to positive. Discouragement gave way to a new hope. They now had a goal in mind, something to look forward to. A team spirit emerged as a result. And, at long last, they got off dead center. It only takes one person with a God-given vision in the home, at the office, or wherever, to make a difference in the outlook and attitude of others. Often, it takes someone new, like Nehemiah, helping us to see things instead of just looking at them.

What about you? Is your need of rebuilding conceivable? Is it believable? If so, then it is achievable. And as you build up your team's spirit, remember that rebuilders say "we" a lot because they are convinced . . . *it's never too late for a new beginning!*

9 STAY ON TRACK

But when Sanballat the Horonite, Tobiah the Ammonite official, and Geshem the Arab heard of it, they laughed at us and despised us, and said, "What is this thing that you are doing? Will you rebel against the king?"

So I answered them, and said to them, "The God of heaven Himself will prosper us; therefore we His servants will arise and build, but you have no heritage or right or memorial in Jerusalem."

—NEHEMIAH 2:19–20

*N*ehemiah was successful in large part because of one word: *focus*. He stayed on track. When we are in the rebuilding process, there will always be those who appear on the scene in an orchestrated attempt to divert us and get us off track. Once the task of rebuilding the wall had begun, Nehemiah was immediately confronted with a group of negative individuals who did their best to divert his focus. They began here in verse 19 of chapter 2, and, throughout the verses following, we will see them from time to time raising their heads until the final stone is placed in the reconstructed wall of Jerusalem.

Nehemiah had a goal that was clearly defined. So, like a fighter pilot, he locked in on his target of rebuilding and focused on staying on track. Those who dedicate themselves to the task of rebuilding learn early on that they cannot and will not please everyone. Sadly, there are some who simply get comfortable living in and around their own ruins. And it is also a fact of life that if you have not met the devil head-on, then you are most likely going the same way he is.

> If you have not met the devil head-on, then you are most likely going the same way he is.

Staying on track is vital to building a team spirit. An interesting example of this occurred during Yogi Berra's playing days when the Yankees were up against the old Milwaukee Braves in the World Series. Yogi was known for his endless chatter while catching behind the plate. He was constantly talking to his own team as well as his opponents. He had a two-fold purpose in doing this: he sought to motivate his fellow teammates, while at the same time, distracting the opposing team's focus. Hank Aaron, the renowned all-time home run leader, stepped up to the plate to bat. Yogi immediately started talking, trying to distract him. "Hank, look at your bat. You are holding it wrong. The trademark is supposed to be face up so you can read it." Aaron never said a word. Yogi kept it up. Then Aaron simply hit the next pitch over the left field fence for a towering home run. After trotting around the bases, as he crossed home plate Aaron looked Berra in the eye and said, "I didn't come here today to read!" Hank Aaron stepped up to the plate with his goal in mind and stayed on track. Some of us have never homered in life because we took our eyes off our goal and got off track.

Nehemiah's example lays out some important steps for us to follow that will enable us to stay on track. First, keep your eyes on the Lord Jesus. Keep your faith in God. As believers, we will not find our ultimate success through our own ability, in those around us, or in some national leader. Listen to Nehemiah's reminder: "The God of heaven Himself will prosper us" (Nehemiah 2:20). This is what keeps us on track in the process of rebuilding. God is with us, and the God of heaven will prosper us.

Next, Nehemiah, this master rebuilder, reminds us to keep a servant's heart. He added, "We His servants . . ." (Nehemiah 2:20). This was his way of reminding us that if we have intentions of being great in God's kingdom then we must be the servant of all. When I came to pastor the historic First Baptist Church in Dallas and began a massive rebuilding process, I kept a verse of Scripture on my desk, on my phone, and on my mirror at home. I looked at it scores of times every day. It was God's promise from 1 Kings 12:7: "If you will be a servant to these people today, and serve them, and answer them, and speak good words to them, then they will be your servants forever." There is nothing that will keep you on track like having a servant's heart.

Still, we must get busy with the task before us: "Therefore, we His servants will arise and build" (Nehemiah 2:20). We are to get busy doing what we already know we should do. We are to get up and build. Staying busy with the task at hand keeps us from getting off track. If you are in sales, then get out there and start making calls. Get busy with your task, and you will not get off track. If you are rebuilding a marriage, get busy with acting as though you're in love, remembering this important truth: it is easier to act your way into a new way of feeling than to feel your way into a new way of acting. Stay focused by keeping your faith in God, having a servant's heart, and getting busy.

Finally, Nehemiah reminds us to see our critics for what they are. Listen to him as he addressed his accusers, "You have no heritage or right or memorial in Jerusalem" (2:20). He boldly confronted his critics and refused to play their game. There are times when leaders must exert a "get tough policy" in the face of some detractors. It goes with the turf. So get ready. If you take up your own task of rebuilding, there will always be a Sanballat or a Tobiah who will come along and try to get you off track. See them for who they are and what they are about. There will be times when some criticism is entirely justi-

> If you take up your own task of rebuilding, there will always be a Sanballat or a Tobiah who will come along and try to get you off track.

fied and should be taken seriously, evaluated, and valued. However, so often, it is there simply to divert your focus from your goal.

Interestingly, Nehemiah did not argue with his detractors. Nor was he in the least bit discouraged by them. He confronted them head-on. Nehemiah was convinced he was doing God's work. He didn't give the time of day to anyone he perceived to be actively opposed to what he knew in his heart was right.

It may be that you are reading these words right now and realize that you have gotten off track. The Lord Jesus Christ wants you on His winning team. He wants to be the rebuilder of anything and everything that may be broken around your life. He has a goal for you, a vision of what He desires you to be. After all, He is our original reminder that . . . *it's never too late for a new beginning!*

PART 3

Rebuilders

Let Go

Without Letting Up

*N*ehemiah is teaching us some valuable lessons on rebuilding. We have been looking, listening, and learning from him as he got started right and then went on to build a team spirit among his troops. We have just left him as the people answered his call to arms with a determined, "Let us rise up and build!" (Nehemiah 2:18). This was not some superficial call to a pumped-up mental attitude or some kind of accelerated hype. These were not idle words. Action was now following attitude. The people were setting their hands to the work (Nehemiah 2:18). The wall was going up. The process of the actual rebuilding was under way.

When studying this Old Testament book of Nehemiah, many readers find it easier to simply skip over chapter 3 and follow the narrative straight from chapter 2 to chapter 4. That's because when you begin reading Nehemiah chapter 3, you immediately notice that it is filled with one boring and unpronounceable name after another. And, for the most part, they are all totally unknown characters in the drama. For example, in just one verse we find this list of people: Hananiah, Shelemiah, Hanun, Meshullam, Berechiah (v. 30). (Just type those words and watch your spell-check go crazy.) These are not your basic household names, even in Old Testament lingo. In fact, most of the many names listed in the third chapter of Nehemiah are never before mentioned in Scripture, nor will they ever be mentioned again. These people only appear on the pages of this chapter for a onetime shot in history. Nehemiah chapter 3 has all the excitement of someone else's boring and lifeless genealogy. In fact, even some biblical commentators completely ignore Nehemiah 3. One well-known and widely read author, in an otherwise fine book on Nehemiah, makes no mention whatsoever of this chapter. It is as if it were never entered into the record. And, a popular publishing company, in its discussion guide accompanying a study of Nehemiah, goes so far as to say, "If your time is limited, this is a better chapter to skip than the others."

However, I am convinced that this third chapter of Nehemiah holds a real key to enabling the work of rebuilding to be completed. Instead of skimming through it quickly, or skipping over it entirely, my contention is that this third chapter of Nehemiah is one of the most important chapters in his entire book. Because it is here that we discover the real secret to Nehemiah's success. Here we see what enabled the work of rebuilding, which had lain dormant for decades, to be completed in just fifty-two days. And what do we find hidden in this chapter? It is the art of delegation. And our friend Nehemiah was the master of it.

Nehemiah *let go without letting up*. And that is the essence of delegation. Upon his return to Jerusalem, Nehemiah knew he could not accomplish this incredible task alone. So after getting off to a good start and building a team spirit, he began to delegate tasks to others. He let go of the ownership of the project's details, but he never let up on his passion or commitment to see it through to completion, and he held others accountable for their tasks along the way.

No matter what we may be attempting to rebuild in and around our lives, learning to delegate is a key to success. In preparation for the writing of this volume, I read not only several commentaries on the book of Nehemiah, but several of the motivational and business books on the market today. Yet this ancient rebuilder in the pages of Scripture has

> No matter what we may be attempting to rebuild in and around our lives, learning to delegate is a key to success.

the most effective recipe for rebuilding to be found anywhere—by far!

I think it is safe to say that Nehemiah learned these
principles of delegation from the Jewish Torah. Earlier,
Moses, himself, demonstrated the necessity of delegation, and he put it into practice quite effectively. He had
become overwhelmed by the challenge of how to deal with
the daily needs of the Israelites, as he led the children of
Israel through their wilderness wanderings. Most of his
valuable time was being taken up with giving personal
advice to the people and judging disputes between them
(see Exodus 18). Jethro, his father-in-law, came upon
the scene and observed how the people were standing in
line all day to seek counsel from Moses. After watching
his son-in-law personally deal with each of them, it was
becoming apparent that, by the end of the day, not only
were the people drained by standing in line for extended
periods, but Moses himself was spent from the endless
counsel. Jethro offered some sage advice that Moses was
wise enough to accept. He encouraged Moses to select
from among the people men who feared God, who were
truthful and respected, and to delegate this task to them.
Thus, Moses began to let go without letting up. He "chose
able men out of all Israel, and made them heads over the
people: rulers of thousands, rulers of hundreds, rulers of

fifties, and rulers of tens" (Exodus 18:25). And the result? The task was completed, not just more efficiently, but more effectively as well.

The passing years did not lessen the importance of this principle of delegation. Jesus, Himself, was the master delegator. He didn't personally feed thousands of people on a Galilean mountainside that day. What did He do? Read John, chapter 6. He had the people sit down in groups. Then, once He had multiplied the loaves and fishes, He distributed them to the twelve disciples, and the twelve then distributed them to the crowds in an orderly progression. The rebuilder who does not discover the principle of delegation—who does not learn to let go without letting up—will never be all that he or she is meant to be.

Another interesting insight emerges when we take the time to read all the dozens of names of those who worked to rebuild the broken wall in Nehemiah chapter three: Nehemiah's name is not one of them. He was a master delegator.

Many people who start out with big dreams of rebuilding never see their wall completed because they have never discovered the art of delegation. Quite honestly, a lot of us confuse *delegate* with *dictate*. "Dictators" lead by

> The rebuilder who does not discover the principle of delegation . . . will never be all that he or she is meant to be.

barking orders and striving to keep everyone under their thumb, always insisting on their way or the highway. These are the "leaders" who not only can't let go, but they also can't let up. The result is lower morale among the troops and a failure to reach their goal. It happens in the home. It happens in the office. It happens on the team and even in the church. Dictators leave no room for team efforts. They give ultimatums, and they squelch innovation and creativity in their efforts to control every little detail. They can't let go, and they can't let up.

And, then, there are those who think that to *delegate* means to *abdicate*. That is, they assign a task, but then they not only let go, they also let up. They have no passion to follow up and hold others accountable. Thus their goals are never accomplished, and their rebuilding tasks are never completed. Abdicators are also usually pretty quick to transfer the blame for failure over to the fellow worker to whom the task was assigned.

For decades, it was my privilege to pastor some wonderful churches. Quite honestly, there are a number of jobs a pastor could do full-time. Studying to preach and teach God's Word several times a week could be a full-time job. Ministering to those in need of comfort and care in large churches with thousands of members could be a full-time job. Counseling those who are troubled, confused, or seeking direction in life could easily fill up a weekly calendar. The daily administration of multimillion-dollar budgets and directing a staff of scores of people could be a full-time job. I have observed some pastors who are so overwhelmed that they begin to dictate to others. I have known others who simply abdicated their place of leadership. The wise leader—whether it's in the church, home, or business—is the one who learns the art of delegation and puts it into practice, who knows how to let things go to other people, but who doesn't let up on the accountability factor.

So how did Nehemiah do it? How was he so successful with such an enormous task, and how was it accomplished in such a short period of time? Nehemiah left us a stellar example to follow by laying out five important principles that are essential to the delegation process: set clear objectives with specific tasks, pick the right person for the right job, be an example yourself, hold others accountable, and be generous in giving genuine pats on the back.

Nehemiah was facing an awesome task. Most rebuilders are. Jerusalem had been lying in rubble for decades. This was no time to dictate and bark orders. Nor was it time to abdicate and leave the work for someone else to finish later. It was time to delegate, to let go without letting up. Nehemiah was successful because he was convinced . . . *it's never too late for a new beginning!*

10   SET CLEAR OBJECTIVES WITH SPECIFIC TASKS

Then Eliashib the high priest rose up with his brethren the priests and built the Sheep Gate; they consecrated it and hung its doors. They built as far as the Tower of the Hundred, and consecrated it, then as far as the Tower of Hananel. Next to Eliashib the men of Jericho built. And next to them Zaccur the son of Imri built.

Also the sons of Hassenaah built the Fish Gate; they laid its beams and hung its doors with its bolts and bars. And next to them Meremoth the son of Urijah, the son of Koz, made repairs. Next to them Meshullam the son of Berechiah, the son of Meshezabel, made repairs. Next to them Zadok the son of Baana made repairs.

—NEHEMIAH 3:1–4

*T*here was no ambiguity about Nehemiah's objective from the beginning. It was crystal clear, and everyone knew it. He was laser-focused on his goal of rebuilding the broken wall and burned-down gates of Jerusalem. He had returned to Jerusalem from Persia, shared his vision with the people, and they had adopted it as their own. He called them to action, and they replied, "Let us rise up and build" (Nehemiah 2:18). Then, in chapter 3, we watch as he assigned them specific tasks. Some were to repair and hang the gates, while others were assigned to work on specific sections of the wall. It was to be a total team effort.

Nehemiah set clear objectives with specific tasks. Each worker knew exactly where he was to be along the wall, what was to be done, and what was expected of each of them. For example, we read, "Eliashib the high priest rose up with his brethren the priests and built the Sheep Gate; they consecrated it and hung its doors. They built as far as the Tower of the Hundred, and consecrated it, then as far as the Tower of Hananel" (3:1). On and on throughout the verses, as they unfold before us, we find Nehemiah setting clear objectives with specific tasks and the people following through.

There were more than two miles of broken-down wall to be repaired, and the task was too large for any one person. That is why Nehemiah divided the wall into forty segments and delegated the work to dozens of leaders along the wall. No wonder this incredible task was completed in record time.

There is a phrase we find recurring over and over

through the verses of Nehemiah chapter three. Nineteen times in these thirty-two verses, we read "next to him" or "after him." Over and over—next to him . . . next to them . . . after him . . . after him . . . after him. All along the wall "next" to each worker and "after" each worker was a fellow worker with his own specific task. These words form a striking picture of unity in the midst of diversity. Men were working next to one another and after one another, in one accord.

One of the all-time great television sitcoms was also one of the real pioneers of that medium. It was called *The Honeymooners*, starring Jackie Gleason. Gleason played the part of Ralph Kramden, an overweight bus driver who lived in an apartment with his wife, Alice. His friend and sidekick was his neighbor Ed Norton, who worked in the sewer department of the local municipality. In one of my favorite episodes, Ralph is trying to get a big piece of furniture through the apartment door. He is sweating profusely and unable to get the heavy object to move. Ed walks by, lunch box in hand, on his way home from work. "Hey, Ralph, can I give you a hand?" he asks. Upon a much-appreciated yes, Ed Norton, clad in his white T-shirt, vest, and rumpled hat, takes hold of the piece of furniture outside the door while Ralph climbs into the apartment through the window and positions himself inside the door. They strain. They pull and push. But the furniture doesn't budge an inch. It is still stuck in the middle of the doorway. This goes on for several minutes. Finally, Ralph stops, wipes his brow with his handkerchief and calls out to Ed through the window, "I don't think we are ever going to get this piece of furniture into this apartment." "Get it in the apartment?" questions Norton. "I thought we were trying to get it out of the apartment!"

> Setting clear objectives with specific tasks is the primary component of the delegation process.

Setting clear objectives with specific tasks is the primary component of the delegation process. Without this first task, there is little hope of completion. Too many have tried to delegate a task to someone else without setting clear objectives, resulting in disaster.

Perhaps you are in need of rebuilding something around your life. What is your objective? Write it out in a sentence, and then decide what tasks need to be done in order to see the objective accomplished. Is there a task you need to take on yourself? Are there others you need to delegate? Be willing to let go, just don't let up. If you have a clear objective and specific tasks, then you are on the way to becoming convinced yourself that . . . *it's never too late for a new beginning!*

11 PICK THE RIGHT PERSON FOR THE RIGHT JOB

Beyond the Horse Gate the priests made repairs, each in front of his own house. After them Zadok the son of Immer made repairs in front of his own house. After him Shemaiah the son of Shechaniah, the keeper of the East Gate, made repairs.

—NEHEMIAH 3:28–29

$\mathcal{P}$icking the right person for the right job is an essential element in the art of delegation. A lot of walls have never been rebuilt because some leader somewhere picked the wrong person for the right job or the right person for the wrong job.

Nehemiah had a knack for picking the right people for the right job. For example, we find him placing people to work along the wall near their own homes. We read, "Benjamin and Hasshub made repairs opposite of their house" (Nehemiah 3:23). Then we read, "Beyond the Horse Gate the priests made repairs, each in front of his own house" (3:28). Nehemiah was smart enough to know that if he assigned the workers close to their own homes, they would take more ownership in the project and more of a personal interest in the detail of the work. They would, no doubt, be a bit more highly motivated to see the job through to completion. And another advantage: no one had to commute to the other side of the city, saving valuable time and energy in the process. Where there appeared to be no one living near certain parts of the wall, Nehemiah would station workers from the outlying towns, like Tekoa and Jericho, who came to assist. He was a wise rebuilder and knew the best place for anyone to start to rebuild a broken wall was near his own home.

Some had the task of removing all the rubbish. Others were busy cutting stones. Some stacked debris to the side, while others laid stones in place along the wall. There was a specific job and a specific place for every person to use his or her own personal gifts and abilities. This principle played out all the way up and down and around the wall of Jerusalem.

One might think the priests would bow out of the rebuilding work in light of their own many temple duties. But to their credit, they each took their place along the wall. And it is interesting to observe where Nehemiah placed them. Their job was to make repairs to the "Sheep Gate" (3:1). This gate would have been of utmost importance to them since it was the very gate through which all the people would enter bringing their sacrifices to the temple for worship.

Nehemiah made sure everyone had a job. Look at this group listed for us in Nehemiah 3. There were goldsmiths who typically spent their days working with intricate, tiny details, and yet they had a place laying stones on the wall (vv. 8, 31–32). Nehemiah recorded that there were men who came from Tekoa and Jericho, more than twenty miles away, to do their part although they had no personal gain to be found in Jerusalem (vv. 2, 5). Everyone got their hands dirty. There were politicians along the wall, along with the VIPs and bigwigs of Jerusalem.

> A lot of walls have never been rebuilt because some leader somewhere picked the wrong person for the right job or the right person for the wrong job.

In chapter 2 of Nehemiah, we see that "the hand of . . . God" was upon them. Now, in chapter 3, we see God working through the hands of the people. They had "set their hands to this good work" (2:18).

As you go about rebuilding your broken wall—whatever it may be—remember that God is the ultimate Rebuilder, and it is He who is truly in control. And somewhere along your wall, God has assigned you a task and a place. You are the right person for the job. Ask God to guide you to the right place, and you'll quickly become convinced that . . . *it's never too late for a new beginning!*

12 BE AN EXAMPLE YOURSELF

So we labored in the work, and half of the men held the spears from daybreak until the stars appeared. At the same time I also said to the people, "Let each man and his servant stay at night in Jerusalem, that they may be our guard by night and a working party by day." So neither I, my brethren, my servants, nor the men of the guard who followed me took off our clothes, except that everyone took them off for washing.

—NEHEMIAH 4:21–23

*W*ise leaders know that they will never get people to follow their lead in the rebuilding process unless they lead by example themselves. This is exactly what Nehemiah did, and, by his own example, he encourages us to do so as well. Even though he omitted his own name in the exhaustive list of workers contained in chapter 3, Nehemiah was a true hands-on leader. He led by example, inspiring his people to work by getting his own hands dirty. He was right there beside them, sweating and working as diligently as any of them. We know this because of what he said in Nehemiah 4:21, 23: "So we labored in the work, and half of the men held the spears from daybreak until the stars appeared. . . . Neither I, my brethren, my servants, nor the men of the guard who followed me took off our clothes, except that everyone took them off for washing."

Recently, while in the beautiful Texas Hill Country, I saw an example of this type of leadership when I witnessed a large flock of geese flying right over me in a V formation, headed south for the winter. There was one who led the way at the point of the formation, and I could hear the others honking encouragement to him as they journeyed along. I became so fascinated by the sight of them that I did some research and found some astonishing leadership principles. The fact is, those geese have a lot to teach us when it comes to leading by example.

First, geese fly in a V formation for a very specific, aerodynamic reason. Each bird, by flapping its wings, creates an uplift for the ones behind it. It is said that a bird flying in formation has three times the flying range of one flying alone. The lesson is obvious: when we are all working together and following the example of the leader, we get to our destination a lot quicker and with much less effort.

> If we had as much sense as a goose, we would keep following the example of our leader and not try to fly it alone.

Another thing I discovered is that

when one of those geese flies out of formation, he immediately meets resistance and hustles back into his place. Here is another lesson that is more than obvious: if we had as much sense as a goose, we would keep following the example of our leader and not try to fly it alone. It just makes the job a lot harder.

I noted something else that day: when the lead goose fell back in formation, another goose immediately flew up to the point to take the lead, following the good example of the first leader. The point is, we all need each other. Everyone should share in the harder work from time to time and be the ones to set the example ourselves.

But the thing that most amazed me was the noise they made as they flew over. They were all honking encouragement to the leader. Then, in my research on these amazing feathered friends, I found another example of encouragement. If one of the geese gets sick or falls out of formation and to the ground, two others peel off and stay with the wounded goose until it either revives or dies. What a lesson! And how much more successful we would be in our own rebuilding jobs if we stuck together like "these birds of a feather."

If we want others to follow our lead, then we must lead by example. This is one of the single greatest principles of effective leadership. It is found not just in a flock of geese, but also all throughout the Bible. In fact, the most poignant and pointed leadership statement to be found anywhere is found in Judges 7:17. Gideon, as he was about to lead his pared-down fighting force out to face the great Midianite army against seemingly insurmountable odds, turned and gave his men a final word: "Do as I do." This may just be the greatest leadership statement ever made. Why? Because people generally end up doing what their leader does. One of my own mentors told me a multitude of times, "Never ask your people to do something you are not doing yourself." Or as Gideon said, "Do as I do"!

Exercising delegation is not about shirking duties. In fact, it is an impossible task unless the leader leads by personal example and carries out his or her own assigned duties. Nehemiah was wise enough to know he would never be able to motivate his troops unless he was down in the trenches with them himself. When we do the same in our own rebuilding process we, too, will become convinced that . . . *it's never too late for a new beginning!*

13 HOLD PEOPLE ACCOUNTABLE

Next to them the Tekoites made repairs; but their nobles did not put their shoulders to the work of their Lord. . . .

Malchijah the son of Harim and Hashub the son of Pahath-Moab repaired another section, as well as the Tower of the Ovens. . . . After them the Tekoites repaired another section, next to the great projecting tower, and as far as the wall of Ophel.

—NEHEMIAH 3:5, 11, 27

*T*alk about holding people accountable for their assigned task . . . Nehemiah knew who worked next to whom and where each of them worked. He knew who did the work, and he also knew who didn't do the work. He recorded for all posterity that "the Tekoites made repairs; but their nobles did not put their shoulders to the work of their Lord" (Nehemiah 3:5). He also took note of those who went above and beyond the call of duty, and he recorded those who "repaired another section" (3:27).

Holding others accountable is essential for anyone

who expects to succeed in the art of delegation. There will always be those who start out in the rebuilding process, but do not finish their specific tasks. This was true of some in Nehemiah's time, and it is still true with us today. After taking note of the neglect by some, Nehemiah simply moved forward with the task ahead and moved with the movers. He stayed on track and remained optimistic in the rebuilding task. He did not allow those who faltered and floundered along the way to discourage him.

Many of us never succeed in rebuilding because the word *accountability* is lost to our vocabulary. This lack of accountability is at the heart of many marriage failures. It is the reason relationships are broken and never healed. It is the reason projects fail. And it also explains why some businesses falter while others flourish.

My wife, Susie, and I, like most of my readers, have an automobile. It is less than two years old at this writing. But twice a year we take it into the dealership to get a checkup and an oil change, not because it was not performing well but because we want to avoid any future problems. We call it preventive maintenance. We also are fortunate enough to own our own home. Recently, we had some repair work done on the roof. It was not leaking, but we noticed some apparent rotting in a few of the rafters. Again, we call it preventive maintenance. I live in a body that happens to be deteriorating with age. Fortunately, nothing is physically wrong with me, but once a year I go in for a complete physical from head to toe. What goes wrong with my car, or my house, or my body usually does so because of one word: *neglect.* No accountability. If accountability is good and works for cars and homes and physical needs, then it is absolutely essential in the process of rebuilding. Rebuilders let go, but they do not let up. They hold the people around them accountable.

Accountability is a part of everyday life. We see it perhaps most obviously in the workplace. After all, we don't just show up to work on Monday at any time we desire. Most of us have to be there at a certain time and work a certain number of hours each day. We are accountable for quotas and goals and deadlines. Businesses that show a profit are successful, in large part, because they hold their employees accountable.

We also see this principle at work every day in local, state, and national government. As citizens, we need laws to govern us and protect us. We need to be held accountable when we run through stoplights and ignore speed limits. Otherwise anarchy would characterize our everyday lives. In our school systems teachers hold students accountable in their studies. They must turn in homework assignments, write papers, and take scheduled tests. No one graduates from any school without being held to the scholastic standards. And what about athletics? Accountability is a huge part of playing sports. If a basketball player commits five personal fouls in the game, he or she is removed from the game. A little closer to home, many of us have home mortgages with scheduled monthly payments. We are responsible for paying them on time. Failing to do so can result in a foreclosure on our home.

When it comes to personal relationships, we all need someone to whom we are accountable. Someone who will remind us of God's standards and give a gentle nudge—or shove—when we stray from those standards. Without such a friend, the result is often self-reliance, self-righteousness, self-sufficiency, and self-centeredness, rather than God-centeredness. This sort of accountability is the "ability" to be open and to allow a small number of trusted friends to speak the truth in love into your life. Nehemiah was wise enough to know that in order to be accountable himself, he had to be *transparent* with true friends and allies, like the king. We all need someone with whom we can open our hearts in honesty and transparency. This vulnerability carries with it the potential to be wounded, but it is both essential and imperative.

> We all need someone with whom we can open our hearts in honesty and transparency.

In an accountability relationship—whether we're the ones being held accountable or the ones holding another accountable—we must also be *reachable*. Everyone needs someone who is close enough to reach out to, someone who is both accessible and approachable. This builds trust and lends validity to the accountability relationship. Those who profit from being held accountable are those who are *teachable*. None of us know everything, and none of us should ever stop learning, especially from those around us. As King Solomon said, "As iron sharpens iron, so a man sharpens the countenance of his friend" (Proverbs 27:17). Finally, those who are accountable must be *truthful* with themselves. Many never enter into accountability relationships because they deceive themselves into thinking that broken relationships are always someone else's fault, and they bear little to no responsibility.

A word of warning: I am not suggesting one should be accountable to those who use criticism, gossip, and judgment as weapons disguised as helpful "critiques." Stay away from those folks. Nehemiah did, and so should we. He could hold his people accountable because they knew he was loyal, affirming, forgiving, and committed to each of the workers stretched along the Jerusalem wall. As King Solomon also said, "Faithful are the wounds of a friend" (Proverbs 27:6). Make sure your friends are good ones.

Nehemiah "wrote the book" on how we can all be successful in the rebuilding process. He held his people accountable. Why? Because Nehemiah knew . . . *it's never too late for a new beginning!*

14 GIVE A GENUINE PAT ON THE BACK

After him Baruch the son of Zabbai carefully repaired the other
section, from the buttress to the door of the house of Eliashib the
high priest.

—NEHEMIAH 3:20

Nehemiah took careful note of what the workers were doing along the wall. Then, in the verses following, we find him going up and down the wall patting his fellow workers on the back with a word of affirmation. There is a recurring phrase woven through the verses of Nehemiah 3. Over and over again, he recognized certain individuals who "repaired another section" (Nehemiah 3:11, 19, 21, 24, 27, 30). He took note not only of who the people were and where they worked, but also what they actually accomplished. And then he wrote it down so that history would remember those who went the second mile. In so doing, Nehemiah developed a tremendous amount of loyalty among his people and built an all-for-one and one-for-all team spirit within them. When it came to delegation, Nehemiah knew the importance of affirmation. He understood that a simple pat on the back was no simple thing.

Nehemiah was not one who was given to playing favorites. Some had bigger, more complex tasks than others. However, he complimented each person on the accomplishment of his or her specific assigned tasks. For example, we read in verse 13 of a group of men and women who worked together to rebuild fifteen hundred feet of broken-down wall. Think about that. It was the length of five football fields. And right next to them, there was a lone individual hard at work on the Refuse Gate who single-handedly repaired it on his own (3:14).

Interestingly, Nehemiah singled out a man by the name of Baruch (3:20). He noted that Baruch "carefully" repaired his assigned section of the wall. In my mind's eye, I can see Nehemiah stopping by his side as he moved along the wall, kneeling down and saying, "Great job! Thank you so much." He made note of this man, Baruch, and here we are twenty-five hundred years later talking about him and the example he sets for us today! Nehemiah was building a spirit of conquest within his team.

There is no greater motivation for those to whom a task is delegated than to hear a word of genuine appreciation, affirmation, and encouragement from their leader.

Unfortunately, we are living in a day of increasing depersonalization and nonverbal communication. With the advent of texts, emails, and social media, we simply don't talk to one another as much anymore. Most of us have become nothing more than a number to a mammoth centralized government, a nameless Social Security number. To the Census Bureau, we are just another statistic. But Nehemiah shows us the power of taking personal interest in those individuals on our team, in our home, at our office, or wherever we may be. Nehemiah treated his coworkers with respect; he knew them and called them by name. He let them know they had worth.

> There is no greater motivation for those to whom a task is delegated than to hear a word of genuine appreciation, affirmation, and encouragement from their leader.

We all need to feel we are valued. Those Jerusalemites working on the wall had been dejected, discouraged, and defeated for their entire lives. Every day for decades, they passed by and looked at that broken wall and those dilapidated, burned-down gates of their city! Like some today, they simply got used to their ruin and rubble and passed by on the other side, accepting it. I am sure, like some of us, they had good intentions and kept telling themselves that someday they were going to do something about those ruins. But "someday" never seemed to come, until, that is, Nehemiah appeared on the scene.

Affirmation is the greatest motivating factor I know of and the single most effective way to keep the rebuilding process moving forward. In the home, children need affirmation. They need to know Dad and Mom believe in them. At the office, workers need to know that the boss values their work and worth and believes in them. At school, the children who learn best are those who know the teacher believes in them. We all are in need of a pat on the back from time to time.

One of the most revealing observations came to me after reading this third chapter of Nehemiah over and over. While mentioning dozens of people by name, Nehemiah never once mentioned his own name—and yet he was the key player. He never said where he worked or what he did. He was too busy going up and down the lines of workers, giving encouragement here and there, a helping hand over there, a pat on the back here, and a whispered word of affirmation there. "We can do this. You are doing great! Keep it up!"

We are halfway through this volume of rebuilding, and it is time that you find your own place along your own wall and begin to do the job that no one else can do as well as you can. Back in Jerusalem, not everyone was supposed to work on the Sheep Gate, but some were. Not everyone was to migrate to the Refuse Gate and repair it, but someone was. There is an assigned task and a special place for each of us along our own wall in the rebuilding process. The sad fact is that some walls in this life are never rebuilt because someone is not in his or her assigned place accomplishing a specific task.

> It is time that you find your own place along your own wall and begin to do the job that no one else can do as well as you can.

The art of delegation is a key, learned behavior in the rebuilding process. This is the way the Lord Jesus Christ has been building His church for two millennia now. He delegates. He has clear objectives and specific tasks for us. He appoints pastors and shepherds. He assigns deacons for servant ministry. He assigns some to be teachers and bestows others with gifts of love and mercy. Each of us has an assigned place in His building, and we each occupy a certain part of His body. He will not dictate to us. And we need not fear He will ever abdicate His throne. We are not puppets. We are people. *His people.* He may let go, but He will never let up. He will never leave nor forsake us. And He wants *you* to know . . . *it's never too late for your own new beginning!*

PART 4

Rebuilders

Understand "YAC"

Is What Really Matters

*T*here is a new acronym in our English vernacular, brought to us from the gridiron of professional football: "YAC." Coined by John Madden, former professional football coach and well-known television analyst, YAC stands for "yards after contact." It is the statistic that measures the success, or lack thereof, of a power running back. Madden began compiling this measurement by counting the number of yards a running back makes after first being hit by an opposing player. It measures the player's ability to keep moving forward toward the goal line after encountering opposition.

Watch for YAC the next time you are viewing a football game. Notice that when a running back first is hit by a player from the opposing team, he doesn't just stop running, throw the ball to the ground, and quit. He doesn't cave in, crumble to the turf, then casually get up, and stroll back to the huddle to regroup and plan the next play. He does not fumble away his opportunity. Nor does he turn around and start running in the opposite direction to avoid more contact. What do the best running backs do? After being hit, they keep moving forward, keep churning their powerful legs, and keep heading in the direction of the goal line. The greatest of the power running backs make most of their yards *after* they meet initial opposition. They score most of their touchdowns *after* they have already been hit. They simply keep going because they know that YAC, yards after contact, is what makes the difference between winning and losing.

> Rebuilders always keep moving forward after they are hit because they have learned that it is the yards after contact that matter most in life, not just in football.

Some of us never rebuild in life because as soon as we are hit with any opposition, we are prone to quit, fumble away our opportunity, or, worse yet, start running in the opposite direction. But rebuilders always keep moving forward after they are hit because they have learned that it is the yards after contact that matter most in life, not just in football. Often, YAC is what determines whether or not we reach our goal, and it is the key element that separates those who rebuild from those who don't.

Chances are pretty good that some who are reading this book right now have stopped rebuilding because they ran into some type of opposition and began to ask, "What is the use?" Perhaps it was a broken relationship that was in the process of rebuilding when conflict came again. Remember: it is the YAC that often makes the difference between success and failure. This is true whether we are be rebuilding our own self-confidence, our marriages, our businesses, or whatever. YAC demonstrates our ability to overcome all obstacles, and it is what separates us from most of the others in the crowd.

Anyone, anywhere, who becomes serious about rebuilding can expect to meet with opposition. Like ham and eggs, steak and potatoes, corn beef and cabbage, and spaghetti and meatballs, rebuilding and opposition go hand in hand. There are times when it comes from without. Some Sanballat or Tobiah will rise up against us as they did against Nehemiah. There are other times when opposition may well up from within our own ranks. Like Nehemiah, we may find that some of our fiercest opposition may actually come from someone who has been on our team. Judah, of all people, was about to give up on Nehemiah and his leadership. But it's how we deal with the opposition—opposition that will surely come—that will largely determine the success or failure of our own rebuilding projects.

In chapter 4 of his book, Nehemiah, like the seasoned

quarterback of a championship team, called four audibles that enabled him to complete the job and reach the goal God had set before him. He kept moving forward after contact. How? By following four key principles:

- First, Nehemiah shows us how important it is to deal with conflict head-on. He didn't ignore it and hope it would just go away. Neither can we turn a blind eye to opposition. Nor can we turn around, run the other way, and expect to see the goal of rebuilding accomplished. We must deal with opposition and conflict head-on.

- Second, Nehemiah made some proper adjustments. There was still a considerable amount of rubbish on and around the broken wall that needed to be removed and hauled away. Any attempt to rebuild the wall on a foundation as shabby as rubbish would only mean that the wall would one day crumble again. From time to time, in our own rebuilding experience, it is necessary for us to call a timeout and make some adjustments to our game plan.

- Third, Nehemiah was an overcomer. Once he had dealt with his opposition head-on and made some proper adjustments to his plan, he overcame obstacles by continuing to do the right thing. He watched, and he worked. With a trowel in one hand and a sword in the other, he continued his rebuilding process, always keeping a keen eye out for any opposition. He never let the opposition deter him from his task ahead. He kept doing what was right.

- Finally, Nehemiah rallied his troops. He knew how important his team's morale was in the rebuilding process. He not only got started with his goal in mind, but now, well into the journey, he continues to work to keep his team focused on that goal.

As we are about to discover, it is the YAC that so often determines the success or failure of the rebuilding project—whatever it may be. Those who make most of their yards *after* contact do so because they truly believe . . . *it's never too late for a new beginning!*

15 DEAL WITH CONFLICT HEAD-ON

But it so happened, when Sanballat heard that we were rebuilding the wall, that he was furious and very indignant, and mocked the Jews. And he spoke before his brethren and the army of Samaria, and said, "What are these feeble Jews doing? Will they fortify themselves? Will they offer sacrifices? Will they complete it in a day? Will they revive the stones from the heaps of rubbish—stones that are burned?"

Now Tobiah the Ammonite was beside him, and he said, "Whatever they build, if even a fox goes up on it, he will break down their stone wall."

Hear, O our God, for we are despised; turn their reproach on their own heads, and give them as plunder to a land of captivity! Do not cover their iniquity, and do not let their sin be blotted out from before You; for they have provoked You to anger before the builders.

So we built the wall, and the entire wall was joined together up to half its height, for the people had a mind to work.

Now it happened, when Sanballat, Tobiah, the Arabs, the Ammonites, and the Ashdodites heard that the walls of Jerusalem were being restored and the gaps were beginning to be closed, that they became very angry, and all of them conspired together to come and attack Jerusalem and create confusion. Nevertheless we made our prayer to our God, and because of them we set a watch against them day and night.

Then Judah said, "The strength of the laborers is failing, and there is so much rubbish that we are not able to build the wall."

—NEHEMIAH 4:1–10

*W*e have walked with and watched Nehemiah as he got started right, built a team spirit, and let go without letting up, but then came his biggest challenge yet—opposition. We should never think just because we are serious about the business of rebuilding that success will come without some type of opposition. In Nehemiah's case, the opposition was persistent (Nehemiah 2:10, 19; 4:1–3, 7–8; 6:1–2). Don't be fooled into thinking that opposition goes away quickly or quietly. As we observed in the preceding pages, Nehemiah, like all great football running backs, knew it was the YAC—the yards after contact—that so often determines success or failure. For that reason, Nehemiah dealt with conflict head-on.

As is usually the case with opposition, Nehemiah's arose from two directions: from without (4:1–3) and from within (4:10). His outside opposition came in the form of mocking and ridicule. When Sanballat heard that

Nehemiah was rebuilding the wall, it infuriated him, and he indignantly "mocked the Jews" (4:1). He then asked, "What are these feeble Jews doing? . . . Will they complete it in a day?" (4:2). Then a man named Tobiah got in his two cents: "Whatever they build, if even a fox goes up on it, he will break down their stone wall" (4:3).

This outside opposition had a threefold plan of attack. First, it was aimed at morale, motives, and mission. In calling Nehemiah's team "feeble Jews," they were attacking the *morale* of his troops. It was an orchestrated attempt to demolish their self-worth and weaken their resolve. When we are in the midst of our own rebuilding process and our own wall is going up, we shouldn't be surprised when someone comes along and attempts to weaken our resolve and demolish our morale.

Next, Nehemiah's *motives* were attacked. Sanballat asserted that Nehemiah and his people were simply doing all this for themselves (4:2), that it was selfish motives that drove them to rebuild. Be wary, fellow rebuilders: there are still many Sanballats around today who never can understand why we would attempt to do something for God's glory alone. When your own motives are questioned, learn from this master rebuilder and just keep doing what is right.

Nehemiah's enemies had attacked morale and

motives, but they were not finished yet. Next, these scoffers attacked the very *mission* behind what moved and motivated Nehemiah toward his goal. They questioned the possibility of his ever being able to finish this enormous task. When Tobiah said, "If even a fox goes up on it, he will break down their stone wall" (4:3), the implication was that rebuilding this wall was just too big a job for such a motley crew to accomplish.

But what was the real issue at stake here? Sanballat and Tobiah didn't like seeing that long-crumbled wall going up again. Habitual critics always resist change. I often wonder about the work of God that never seems to cause the enemy to lift its head or raise its hand in opposition. The truth is that anytime we take God at His word and begin a rebuilding work that will honor Him, we can expect to see a Sanballat or a Tobiah show up to mock, ridicule, and attack, not only our morale, but our motives and mission as well. For example, the best way to rebuild the walls of a crumbling marriage is for the husband and wife to assume the spiritual roles set out for them repeatedly in the Scripture. God designed the home to have a head. He created husbands and wives to love each other sacrificially, as Christ loved, and yet plainly revealed that the husband should be the head of the wife as "Christ is the head of the church" (Ephesians 5:23). But tell this to our modern world and get ready for the mocking and ridicule that will come your way when biblical truth is expressed and applied to our lives. Expect opposition

> Habitual critics always resist change.

to come from without, and be ready to do as Nehemiah did: deal with conflict head-on.

Opposition not only comes from without; it comes from within as well (Nehemiah 4:10). And it is this opposition from within that can so often be the most devastating. The fact was that the tribe of Judah didn't deal well with outside opposition. They were just about ready to give up and give in. Judah even said, "The strength of the laborers is failing, and there is so much rubbish that we are not able to build the wall" (4:10). Of all people—Judah! Judah was the strongest of all the twelve tribes of Israel, of whom the Bible says, "The scepter shall not depart from Judah, nor a lawgiver from between his feet, until Shiloh comes" (Genesis 49:10). Judah was the very tribe from which the Messiah, the "Lion of the tribe of Judah" (Revelation 5:5), would eventually come. This opposition from one of Nehemiah's key players must have been like a dagger in his heart.

So what happened to the people of Judah? It is obvious from their statement—fatigue, frustration, and potential failure were affecting them. *Fatigue* led the way and contributed to their frustration—it usually does. "The strength of the laborers is failing," they said. The people had been working so hard at their assigned task that they had become tired and physically depleted. Remember: we are not talking about just stacking up a few small bricks here. Anyone who has ever journeyed to the Holy Land—or seen pictures of it—cannot help but be amazed when they see just how massive these stones are that make up the wall of Jerusalem. No wonder the people's strength was failing, and it's no wonder their fatigue was moving them to discouragement. The fatigue factor is often at the root of many of our own failures. We simply give out and become too tired to go on, so we are then tempted to give in and to give up. When fatigue sets in during the rebuilding process, it brings along with it a loss of perspective, and little things often become much bigger than they really are.

Frustration followed the people's fatigue. Judah said, "There is so much rubbish." The massive piles of debris made the magnitude of the task seem virtually impossible. There was just so much to be done. The people were losing their vision and the enthusiasm they needed to complete their task. Fatigue pulled their focus from their goal and placed it upon the rubbish, which led to frustration. Those who are in the process of rebuilding are often tempted by this very same thing. There are times when it is so easy to focus on the sheer magnitude of our own task, allowing frustration to set in just as it did with Judah.

When fatigue and frustration are coupled together, then *failure* is not far behind. Judah was not through with his opposition yet. "We are not able to build the wall," he declared. The people had lost their confidence to continue. Perhaps you are reading these words and find yourself saying this same thing. You started out with great intentions, but then fatigue came, which led to frustration. And now you find yourself repeating Judah's words of failure: "I am not able to build the wall."

At this point, it serves us well to remember where the Jews were in their own rebuilding process: "So we built the wall, and the entire wall was joined together up to half its height" (Nehemiah 4:6). They were at the halfway point. It was halftime. This is a dangerous place in our own rebuilding processes. In fact, it can be the most discouraging point along the journey. Halftime comes to each of us. Our wall is halfway rebuilt, when suddenly we become aware that we are not where we had intended to be at this point in our journey. So we, like Judah, are tempted to give up and conclude we "are not able to build" our wall. It's at this point we must remember that it is the yards after contact that really matter and that will ultimately bring us success.

Notice that our opposition from within often shows up

in the form of the word *but*. "Yes, it is true we have built half the wall," Judah essentially says, "*but* there is too much rubbish to finish it." How many times have we heard someone agree with us up to a certain point and then add *but*? "That is a great idea, *but* I don't think it can be done." "That is a wonderful suggestion, *but* it has never been done before." "That is an intriguing thought, *but* we don't have enough resources." The next time someone says something similar to you, stop and remember this: everything that person said before the *but* is very likely what he or she doesn't really believe, and everything he or she says after the *but* is most likely how he or she truly feels about the situation.

The Lord Jesus, Himself, was not immune to opposition from within His own closely knit band of followers. Simon Peter tried to divert Him from the cross right after making his great confession. And what about Judas Iscariot? But meeting with opposition isn't necessarily a bad thing. It can actually confirm that we are on the right track. Because when we are in the process of rebuilding something good, and we do not meet with demons of opposition, then it is most likely because we are going the same way they are. And that is not good.

> When fatigue and frustration are coupled together, then *failure* is not far behind.

Put yourself in Nehemiah's place

when he was confronted with the negativity of Judah. How would you respond? What kind of yards after contact would you achieve? Now think about what Nehemiah did: he dealt with the conflict head-on. He persisted in his task. He just kept mixing the mortar. He kept laying the stones. He kept rebuilding the wall. I am sure it would have been much easier for him to go back to Persia and get his old cushy job back without all the headaches. But he never gave that a thought. Rebuilding the broken wall of Jerusalem, or our own for that matter, is God's project, not Nehemiah's, and not our own.

Despite the opposition, Nehemiah kept making yards after contact. And the more he moved toward his goal, the more the opposition increased. The enemy "became very angry, and all of them conspired together to come and attack Jerusalem and create confusion" (4:7–8). These warring factions now joined together to form a conspiracy against Nehemiah. There is an old Arab proverb that is in play here and has proven itself true down through the centuries: "The enemy of my enemy is my friend." Even the Lord Jesus watched as this principle played out before Him. The Bible records, "That very day Pilate and Herod became friends with each other, for previously they had been at enmity with each other" (Luke 23:12). Our Savior bore the brunt of this evil conspiracy.

Note that Nehemiah first began to meet his opposition head-on in prayer: "We made our prayer to our God, and because of them we set a watch against them day and night" (Nehemiah 4:9). First, Nehemiah prayed, and then he continued the work. For Nehemiah, prayer was a priority, but it was not a substitute for action. And so it should be with us. For example, are you seeking to rebuild a vocation? First pray, and then go fill out those applications, beat the pavement, and make your contacts. Are you trying to rebuild a marriage? First pray, and then say you are sorry and begin to act as you did when you first fell in love.

Nehemiah knew it was the YAC—the yards after contact—that would see him through to the completion of his task. So he dealt with conflict and opposition head-on. He didn't quit. He didn't fumble the ball. He didn't run off in the opposite direction. He kept moving toward his goal. The mark of the accomplished rebuilder is that he or she deals with conflict head-on. Rebuilders have an optimism that is contagious, and they persevere in the face of opposition.

Yes, John Madden had it right. It is the YAC that truly makes the difference in life. Even though you may be hit with opposition right now, keep moving forward and keep focused on your goal because . . . *it's never too late for a new beginning!*

16   MAKE PROPER ADJUSTMENTS

Then Judah said, "The strength of the laborers is failing, and there is so much rubbish that we are not able to build the wall."

And our adversaries said, "They will neither know nor see anything, till we come into their midst and kill them and cause the work to cease."

So it was, when the Jews who dwelt near them came, that they told us ten times, "From whatever place you turn, they will be upon us."

Therefore I positioned men behind the lower parts of the wall, at the openings; and I set the people according to their families, with their swords, their spears, and their bows. And I looked, and arose and said to the nobles, to the leaders, and to the rest of the people, "Do not be afraid of them. Remember the Lord, great and awesome, and fight for your brethren, your sons, your daughters, your wives, and your houses."

—NEHEMIAH 4:10–14

I was in the stands and personally watched one of the most amazing sporting events of all time—the greatest comeback in college football bowl history. It took place at the Alamo Bowl in 2016 between Oregon and Texas Christian University (TCU), both ranked in the top ten nationally. Playing with a quarterback who had never before started in a major college football game, TCU found themselves down 31–0 at halftime. Many of their fans had given up hope and had headed for the exits. Hundreds of thousands of television viewers across the country changed the channel or just turned off their televisions. However, there was one person who still believed, who still held to the hope of a comeback even when the situation looked so bleak. Coach Gary Patterson took his team into the locker room at halftime and made some *proper adjustments*. He changed the defensive scheme. He instilled within his team the attitude that it was never over until it was over. Then he turned to his inexperienced quarterback, Bram Kohlhausen, whose father had recently died. The coach looked into the young man's face and said, "Your dad has passed away, but he is watching. Can you imagine if you came back? Can you come back? Can you go out there and win this football game?" By the time halftime ended, the TCU players practically broke the locker room door down trying to get back on the field.

The result of those halftime adjustments was amazing. Oregon didn't score again in the third or fourth quarters, and Kohlhausen led his team to tie the game 31–31 at the end of four quarters. Then, in triple overtime, he himself scored to complete the greatest comeback victory in bowl history. And all because a coach didn't give up when he met stiff opposition but instead made some proper adjustments.

Nehemiah was something of a coach himself, and he knew it was the YAC, the yards after contact, that would determine whether his team would win or lose. So he, too, made some proper adjustments at halftime when the wall was halfway completed. He put his finger on the problem of the opposition he was facing. Some of the Jews were dwelling too near the enemy (Nehemiah 4:12). And the problem was that those from the tribe of Judah had been listening to those Jews who lived close to the enemy. The enemy was influencing them with their negativity. Being far removed from the center glow of the dynamic rebuilding spirit, they were picking up on the gossip of those who sought to discourage them. Living so near the enemy caused them to alter their focus and place their immediate attention on the enemy itself. They began to listen to the scoffers instead of listening to their God. This can happen to people who are in the process of rebuilding their lives. They can find themselves dangerously close to those who are attempting to discourage them, and they can begin to listen to them instead of moving themselves nearer to the center of where God is rebuilding.

One of Judah's primary concerns and complaints was that there was "so much rubbish" (4:10). There was nothing wrong with the actual foundation upon which Nehemiah and his team were rebuilding their wall. It was rock-solid. The problem existed because for years all types of junk and debris had accumulated on top of that foundation. Any attempt to rebuild the wall without first removing the rubbish would have been frustrating and futile. Oh, they may have gotten the wall up, and it may even have looked really good, but the first big assault of any kind would have brought it tumbling down once again. It is always dangerous to attempt to rebuild a wall on a foundation as unstable as rubbish. Yet there are many who attempt this today, especially when it comes to trying to rebuild a relationship. Relational rubbish has a way of accumulating untouched over the years. To not remove it and to attempt to build again on top of it only assures that in a short time that relationship will crumble again. Relational rubbish can only be removed through true repentance and unconditional forgiveness.

Many of us who are in need of

> Relational rubbish can only be removed through true repentance and unconditional forgiveness.

rebuilding already have a solid foundation. We do not need to lay a new one. But we do need to remove our own accumulated rubbish so the solid foundation can be exposed once again. Many marriages have been built on a solid foundation, but it is the rubbish that has been allowed to pile up across the years that is the problem. We need to remove it, to get back to the foundation, and to make our own proper adjustments when we meet opposition.

Others of us are living lives that were originally built on a solid foundation. We were brought up on the principles of honor, decency, and integrity that are rooted in the Bible. The problem lies in the fact that those principles have not been seen in a while because all the rubbish of life has buried them. And, unfortunately, some of us continue to attempt to build on that rubbish, instead of first removing it. This perpetuates an endless cycle of rebuilding and collapse, and it is a major reason why more walls of life are not solidly and permanently rebuilt.

When Nehemiah met with opposition, he first faced it head-on, and then he made the proper adjustments needed to complete the task. Listen to him, like a motivating coach at halftime, as he regrouped his troops: "Do not be afraid of them. Remember the Lord, great and awesome, and fight for your brethren, your sons, your daughters, your wives, and your houses" (4:14).

It was halftime for Nehemiah, and the wall was at half its height (4:6). It was time to make the proper adjustments to the game plan. Nehemiah called all his people off the wall, rallied them together, huddled them up, gave them an inspiring challenge, and then sent them out to get rid of the rubbish and finish strong. Like a seasoned coach of a championship team, he made the necessary halftime adjustments. There was a rebuke—"Do not be afraid of them." He addressed their fears and encouraged them—"Remember the Lord, great and awesome." Then he exhorted them—"Fight for your brethren."

Are any of us wondering why we rebuild only to see our walls crumble again time after time? Could it be that we are attempting to rebuild on a foundation as shiftless as rubble? Remember, it is the YAC that matters. And sometimes opposition comes in the form of debris that first needs to be removed. As we remove that debris—through personal repentance and unconditional forgiveness—and as we continue moving forward toward our goal, we will become more and more convinced of the fact that . . . *it's never too late for a new beginning!*

17 KEEP DOING WHAT IS RIGHT

And it happened, when our enemies heard that it was known to us, and that God had brought their plot to nothing, that all of us returned to the wall, everyone to his work. So it was, from that time on, that half of my servants worked at construction, while the other half held the spears, the shields, the bows, and wore armor; and the leaders were behind all the house of Judah. Those who built on the wall, and those who carried burdens, loaded themselves so that with one hand they worked at construction, and with the other held a weapon. . . . So we labored in the work, and half of the men held the spears from daybreak until the stars appeared. At the same time I also said to the people, "Let each man and his servant stay at night in Jerusalem, that they may be our guard by night and a working party by day." So neither I, my brethren, my servants, nor the men of the guard who followed me took off our clothes, except that everyone took them off for washing.

—NEHEMIAH 4:15–17, 21–23

*C*onvinced that it was the YAC, yards after contact, that would bring success, Nehemiah dealt with conflict head-on and made the necessary proper adjustments. Then, he simply moved toward his goal by keeping on doing what he knew was right. He framed it this way: "All of us returned to the wall, everyone to his work" (Nehemiah 4:15).

There is an important principle we see at play in these verses of chapter 4: Nehemiah never left the building for the battle! That bears repeating—Nehemiah never left the focus of building his wall for the fight of the battle. When opposition arises, the temptation all too often is to leave the rebuilding process and plunge headlong into the battle. And it would have been easy for Nehemiah to answer the scorn that came his way with scorn of his own—but he refused. Wisely, he and his team "returned to the wall" and kept doing what was right.

Here we see a prime example of someone making yards after contact. The opposition was mocking, but Nehemiah was rebuilding. The opposition was ridiculing, but he kept doing what was right. They threatened repeatedly, but he kept moving forward. They despised him, but he kept mixing mortar and laying stones. They conspired against him, but the wall kept rising upward.

Maintaining the focus to keep doing what is right in

the face of opposition is a powerful principle. Note that half of Nehemiah's people watched while the other half worked. Half of them held spears for their defense and half of them held trowels for their mortar. To keep doing what is right is one of the greatest secrets to successful rebuilding, no matter what we need to rebuild around us.

The apostle Paul also knew the power of this principle. He led the entire league when it came to yards after contact. He was stoned at Lystra and left for dead, shipwrecked at Malta, repeatedly imprisoned, and severely beaten, and yet he kept doing what he knew was right. Listen to a portion of his letter to those in Corinth: "We are hard-pressed on every side, yet not crushed; we are perplexed, but not in despair; persecuted, but not forsaken; struck down, but not destroyed" (2 Corinthians 4:8–9). Paul was saying to them and to us, "I get right back up and keep doing what is right."

All throughout these pages of Nehemiah 4, we have observed him, time after time, leading by his own example. Now halftime has come and along with it some seemingly insurmountable opposition. But Nehemiah didn't give in or give up. Instead, he doubled up and kept doing the right thing. Throughout it all, he stood shoulder to shoulder with his team. Great leaders are known for this worthy trait. He led his people all those years ago, and now, across all these centuries, he leads you and me by his example. He challenges us to return to our own wall, make some proper adjustments, and simply keep on doing the right thing. Because those who really understand the principle of YAC also understand that . . . *it's never too late for a new beginning!*

18   RALLY THE TROOPS

Every one of the builders had his sword girded at his side as he built. And the one who sounded the trumpet was beside me.

Then I said to the nobles, the rulers, and the rest of the people, "The work is great and extensive, and we are separated far from one another on the wall. Wherever you hear the sound of the trumpet, rally to us there. Our God will fight for us."

—NEHEMIAH 4:18–20

We all are in need of a Nehemiah to encourage us along the way in our own rebuilding processes. Had it not been for the consistent encouragement of Nehemiah, the Jews would have abandoned their task, leaving the wall in shambles as they had done all those years before. But this time it was different. The presence of one individual, wholly committed to the task, was now rallying all the troops.

During the darkest days of World War II and after the bombing of London left much of the city center in shambles, Winston Churchill, the wartime prime minster, kept these words on a small placard on his war room desk:

"Please understand there is no depression in this house and we are not interested in the possibilities of defeat—they do not exist." It was a similar mentality that moved and motivated Nehemiah some two and a half millennia before Churchill. One person can make an amazing difference in the rebuilding process when he or she truly believes that the possibility of defeat does not exist. Nehemiah believed, and so can you!

Nehemiah had a rallying point for his entire team. He kept the trumpeter always close and constantly at his side. He instructed his troops, "Wherever you hear the sound of the trumpet, rally to us there. Our God will fight for us" (Nehemiah 4:20). Don't miss this picture. All along the circumference of the wall, the workers were scattered. In some places the ranks were thin. At the sound of the trumpet, they were to leave their work and rally around Nehemiah for the overthrow of the enemy. No one was to be left to face the enemy alone. The focal point of this whole strategy was Nehemiah, their leader.

Across our world today, there are all kinds of men and women aiding in the rebuilding process. There are preachers, laborers, missionaries, teachers, and laypersons scattered all along the wall. As in Jerusalem, in some places the ranks are spread very thin. Some are way out there, living extremely close to all sorts of enemies of the gospel. Others are cut off from fellowship with those they love, but they keep rebuilding. But we all have our own Commander in Chief, the Lord Jesus Christ, and He is the rallying point for any and all of us who are engaged in the process of rebuilding. One day we will hear His trumpeter give the sound. We will lay down our tools, leave our work, and rally around Him. But until then, like Nehemiah, we must continue the rebuilding process. We must keep overcoming our obstacles and our opposition. How? By dealing with conflict head-on. By making some proper adjustments. By keeping on doing what is right and by rallying those around us to do the same.

I attended a basketball game recently where the home team had a huge, seemingly insurmountable lead going into the final quarter of play. Then, suddenly, the momentum changed, and the lead began to dwindle. With just a couple of minutes left in the game, the coach called a time-out. He made some proper adjustments, encouraged his team to keep doing what was right by playing their assigned positions, and then he rallied them around him to finish strong. They did, and they won. It may be that some of us need to call our own time-out in life to rally our troops.

In verse 20, Nehemiah reminded his team, "Our God will fight for us." Sanballat and Tobiah had said, "You won't." Judah had said, "We can't." But Nehemiah said, "God will!" People have a way of rallying around a cause if they are convinced that God is in the midst of it. Which voice do the troops hear from your mouth? Is it the voice of Sanballat and "We won't"? Is it the voice of Judah and "We can't"? Or is it the voice of Nehemiah and "God will!"? Nehemiah chose to proclaim, "God will!" And He did! Just look at verse 15 of chapter 6, "So the wall was finished . . . in fifty-two days." That is some phenomenal yardage after contact! And for us today, it still comes down to how we, ourselves, rate in YAC—yards after contact—that will determine the success of our own rebuilding efforts.

> People have a way of rallying around a cause if they are convinced that God is in the midst of it.

In the early days of my time as pastor of the First Baptist Church in Dallas, I often felt overwhelmed. Before me was the tremendous challenge of "rebuilding" one of the great, historic churches of America. At the time, my daughter, Holly, was playing point guard on the high school basketball team at our First Baptist Academy. I would constantly encourage her to take more shots and to drive for the basket with abandon. If I told her once, I told her ten thousand times, "You can't score if you don't shoot. You will miss 100 percent of the shots you never take."

Then there came a particularly low moment in my ministry a year or so later, when I began to feel a bit like Judah, wondering if there was so much rubbish needing to be removed that my God-assigned task was insurmountable. But then a postcard came in the mail one morning. It was from Holly, who by this time was immersed in her freshman year at the university. The card simply said, "Daddy, remember . . . you will miss 100 percent of the shots you never take. I believe in you. Love, Holly." It stayed on my credenza all the remaining years of that wonderful and fruitful pastorate there in Dallas.

It may well be that some reader is tempted to give up on the rebuilding process. Instead, take a time-out. Remember your coach is Christ Himself. He is coaching you up, encouraging you to deal with conflict head-on, guiding you to make some necessary and proper adjustments, and strengthening you to keep on doing what is right. He is rallying the troops around you, and you and I are on His team.

Long before John Madden ever coined the phrase, Nehemiah shows us the importance of YAC. He is not speaking softly to us across the centuries. He is shouting now, "Keep going! Don't quit. Don't fumble. Take the shot. Don't give up and run the other way. Keep moving forward. You will miss 100 percent of the shots you never take!" Nehemiah also shows us the importance of rallying the troops as you keep moving forward with your goal in sight because . . . *it's never too late for a new beginning!*

PART 5

Rebuilders

Never Cut

What They Can Untie

During my childhood days, we had a vacant lot that became the gathering place for all the neighborhood kids. We had some great ball games on that old vacant lot. It was like Yankee Stadium to me and my pals on Crenshaw Street. Recently, I drove through that old neighborhood on the east side of Fort Worth. The houses and yards that once were so manicured and pristine are mostly unkempt and in disrepair these days. In fact, several of the houses on my block are vacant and boarded up, and the ones still inhabited have iron bars over the windows and doors. But the old vacant lot is still there in all its former glory. As I parked in front of it, a thousand memories flooded my mind.

There was one particular kid on our street who always showed up at the lot to play ball with us. He always wore black high-top canvas tennis shoes laced only about halfway up, leaving several empty eyelets at the top of his shoes. In the library of people I have known who were impatient, this kid was way up there on the top shelf. When his shoe-laces became knotted, he never took the time, nor had the patience, to sit down and patiently work the knots out so the laces could be untied. He would ceremoniously take out his little pocketknife and cut the knot off, taking with it several inches of shoestrings. Thus, his shoes never had enough laces to reach all the way to the top.

As I read and studied the fifth chapter of Nehemiah, I thought about that kid and came to this conclusion: rebuilders never cut what they can untie. Think about that statement. Rebuilders patiently work through the knots of interpersonal relationships instead of just cutting them off and going on about life. They take their time, making sure the knots are untied in such a way that they can be tied once again. It is a fact: rebuilders never cut what they can untie.

> It is a fact: rebuilders never cut what they can untie.

Conflict resolution is a hot topic these days, in both the business world and the social arena. And it should be. Conflict can tear your team apart—whether it is in the home, at the office, on the court, or even in the church. Unresolved conflict can do irreparable damage. Here is another fact: wherever you find two people, you also often find the need for effective conflict resolution. Some men and women have lost their jobs because they never discovered the secrets of conflict resolution. They simply move their way through life, continually cutting off what they could have easily untied. I know churches that have split right down the middle because of this. As a pastor, I have watched homes break up because too many husbands and wives found it easier to simply cut away what could have been untied with some effort. Yes, disagreements are inevitable in life, but they don't have to be destructive.

Nehemiah 5 finds the Jews faced with the very real possibility that the wall might not be rebuilt due to some conflicts that had arisen between members of Nehemiah's own team. The success of our own rebuilding projects is largely determined by the manner in which we learn to resolve the conflicts that come knocking. We can do everything else according to plan. However, if we continue to cut what we could be untying, we will never see our own rebuilding process through to successful completion.

This is also true with those who are seeking to rebuild broken relationships. Relationships, like shoelaces, can be tied again if they are not severed. If we have any hope of rebuilding, we must leave our pocketknives in our pockets and avoid the temptation to whip them out and lop off the gnarled knots of twisted relationships. Successful rebuilders know this. When tensions build up, it takes patience and perseverance, determination and dedication to untie tense situations. And these are exactly the sorts of skills we are about to observe Nehemiah using.

The story unfolds before us in the early verses of chapter 5 when the people stopped their work on the wall and began arguing with one another. At the same time they were stacking up a physical wall around Jerusalem, they were also stacking up an invisible wall of resentment between themselves. Nehemiah was then faced with an escalating situation that threatened to quickly spiral out of control and divert the focus of rebuilding.

The conflict that arose was precipitated by a severe famine that forced many of the workers to mortgage their homes and belongings (5:3). Taxes were choking the very life and sustenance out of them (5:4). And, if that were not bad enough, their own Jewish brothers, who had loaned them money in their time of need, were charging them outlandish interest rates on their loans, making them virtually impossible to repay. As one can imagine, this was wreaking havoc on the morale of the rebuilders along the wall. It is no wonder that Nehemiah became "very angry" (5:6). The situation desperately needed someone skilled in the art of conflict resolution. Because if this conflict could not be resolved, the ultimate goal of rebuilding the broken wall would never be accomplished. It was a critical time in the entire rebuilding effort.

Nehemiah knew this was no time to cut what could be untied. This skillful people person began to untie the knots of conflict and resolve the problems so that everyone could get back to the task of rebuilding. This led to the ultimate conclusion we find in Nehemiah 6:15, "So the wall was finished . . . in fifty-two days."

In chapter 5, Nehemiah systematically demonstrates four valuable principles that, when put into practice, can have the same positive results in our own experience that they had in his. Long centuries before any of the modern motivational gurus wrote on conflict resolution, Nehemiah employed four essential and now time-tested elements of conflict resolution:

- There is a time to back off.
- There is a time to stand up.
- There is a time to give in.
- And there is a time to reach out.

You will never find successful rebuilders cutting what they can untie, because they know . . . *it's never too late for a new beginning!*

19

THERE IS A TIME TO BACK OFF

And there was a great outcry of the people and their wives against their Jewish brethren. For there were those who said, "We, our sons, and our daughters are many; therefore let us get grain, that we may eat and live."

There were also some who said, "We have mortgaged our lands and vineyards and houses, that we might buy grain because of the famine."

There were also those who said, "We have borrowed money for the king's tax on our lands and vineyards. Yet now our flesh is as the flesh of our brethren, our children as their children; and indeed we are forcing our sons and our daughters to be slaves, and some of our daughters have been brought into slavery. It is not in our power to redeem them, for other men have our lands and vineyards."

And I became very angry when I heard their outcry and these words. After serious thought, I rebuked the nobles and rulers, and said to them, "Each of you is exacting usury from his brother." So I called a great assembly against them.

—NEHEMIAH 5:1–7

$\mathcal{N}$ehemiah began the whole process of conflict resolution by, first, backing off. And there was a wise reason to do so. He had, in his own words, become "very angry" (Nehemiah 5:6). Yet he (unlike some of us in similar situations) was wise enough to know that when anger rises up in our hearts, the best thing we can do to avoid further conflict is to back off and give some "serious thought" (5:7) to the situation.

Nehemiah's initial response to the conflict that had arisen on his team was anger. He readily admitted it. In fact, he even recorded it in these memoirs for all posterity to read. He didn't try to conceal his anger. He made no excuses for it. He didn't act as if it didn't exist. He did not try to minimize it. He didn't couch it in language that sought to disguise it as something else. Nor did he attempt to repress it. He simply admitted it. In his own words, "I became very angry" (5:6).

This righteous indignation, which he called anger, stemmed from the fact that his people were engaged in acts against one another that were diametrically opposed to the teachings of their holy Scripture, the Torah. The Jewish Torah expressly taught that if one lent money to his people who were poor, then he should not charge them interest (Leviticus 25:35–38). In Deuteronomy we read, "To your brother you shall not charge interest, that the

LORD your God may bless you in all to which you set your hand" (23:20). Nehemiah was angry because his people knew better. They were knowingly and blatantly disobeying God's clear teaching, which, in turn, was causing increasing dissension in the ranks of his workers. If not stopped, this would ultimately lead to the dissolution of their goal of rebuilding the wall.

So Nehemiah pulled no punches. He was hot about it. But, at the same time, he was also very wise. Instead of rushing in to confront those in the wrong, he backed off to give himself time to think. Some of our own conflicts are never resolved because we don't back off and take time to think. Instead we rush in, armed with clever ways of excusing our anger. Then we are quick to exclaim, "You made me act like that. You know where my hot button is, and you enjoy pushing it." Too often, we avoid personal responsibility by implying someone else is to blame for our own outbursts. Others simply repress their anger. But like a cancer eating away at the body, repressed anger turns to bitterness. Nehemiah did neither of those things. He freely admitted his anger. There was no doubt about the fact that he was upset. But, in the very next verse, he immediately did a very wise thing—*he backed off.*

Many people tend to barge right into the midst of the conflict and, in their anger, only succeed in agitating the matter further. By so doing, they cut what they could have untied. Nehemiah's anger in verse 6 and his rebuke at the end of verse 7 are the sandwich ends of his backing off to give "serious thought" to the conflict.

Verse 7 tells us that Nehemiah gave this situation "serious thought." This phrase in our English Bible translates two Hebrew words meaning "to counsel or to give advice" and "the inner man." This latter word is actually translated "heart" more than five hundred times in the Old Testament. Nehemiah is literally saying, "I backed off and listened to my heart. I took counsel with my heart." Listening to our hearts is a wise practice for all of us to adopt. Instead of speaking first in anger, how many more conflicts might be resolved if we first backed off and just listened to what God was saying to our hearts in His still, small voice?

> Instead of speaking first in anger, how many more conflicts might be resolved if we first backed off and just listened to what God was saying to our hearts in His still, small voice?

This principle of backing off is found laced throughout the fabric of the Bible. Remember Habakkuk? Backing off is what he practiced when he, too, became angry. God was allowing the Babylonians to swoop down upon Jerusalem and ultimately destroy the city and demolish its wall. But we find Habakkuk backing off and climbing up in a watchtower to "watch to see what [God] will say to me" (Habakkuk 2:1).

When Nehemiah stepped back, it was to give himself some time to think through the situation and get everything in proper perspective. By backing off and listening to his heart, he found a course of action that ultimately led his people back up on the wall and back to the business of rebuilding. In spite of the conflict and in spite of his own anger over it, Nehemiah never lost sight of his ultimate goal and purpose: to complete the task of rebuilding the broken wall of Jerusalem. Too often, in our own anger, we shoot from the hip and speak without thinking, and, in so doing, fail in our attempts to resolve our conflicts. Have you ever been tempted to send a text or an email in anger? Don't do it. Why? Because then you never have to take back something you never should have said! Instead, back off and listen to your heart. Wait a day or two. It will save a lot of heartache and ill will, and it make your knots so much easier to untie later on.

Rebuilders never cut what they can untie. They realize that when anger arises, it is a signal to back off and listen to their hearts. They take time to give "serious thought" to the process of conflict resolution. When we back off and listen to our hearts, it becomes easier to see that . . . *it's never too late for a new beginning!*

20

THERE IS A TIME TO STAND UP

*After serious thought, I rebuked the nobles and rulers, and said
to them, "Each of you is exacting usury from his brother." So
I called a great assembly against them. And I said to them,
"According to our ability we have redeemed our Jewish brethren
who were sold to the nations. Now indeed, will you even sell
your brethren? Or should they be sold to us?"*

*Then they were silenced and found nothing to say. Then I
said, "What you are doing is not good. Should you not walk in
the fear of our God because of the reproach of the nations, our
enemies?"*

—NEHEMIAH 5:7–9

After Nehemiah spent valuable time backing off,
he then moved to the next step in conflict resolution: there is a time to stand up. And that is exactly
what he did. Nehemiah boldly stood up and confronted
those he believed to be in the wrong and whose actions
had initiated the conflict. "I rebuked the nobles and
rulers, and said to them, 'Each of you is exacting usury

from his brother'" (Nehemiah 5:7). Nehemiah "rebuked" the elders and brought them face-to-face with the point of contention—they were charging interest to their own Jewish brothers who were in financial need, and in so doing brought "reproach" (5:9) upon the people of God.

It is important to note that conflict resolution never means backing off and giving in at any cost. Nehemiah was a strong and effective leader. After backing off to listen to his heart, he stood up and rebuked those who were in the wrong. Conflict resolution is never simply another form of pacifism.

One afternoon on a grassy green hillside on the northern shore of the Sea of Galilee, Jesus addressed this very point in His well-known and often quoted Sermon on the Mount. He pronounced a blessing on the "peace*makers*" (Matthew 5:9, emphasis added), not the "peace *lovers.*"

Yes, we should love peace, but we should not seek it at the cost of sacrificing what we know to be right. There are times when nations and individuals have to "make peace" by standing up and not just backing off.

> Conflict resolution is never simply another form of pacifism.

One example of a person who cared enough to confront is found in a man named Nathan. Most of us remember the well-known Bible story of King David lusting after a lady named Bathsheba so that he eventually committed adultery with her and sent her husband into battle, where he was killed. He didn't want his family or friends to find out about it. Like so many today, he was foolish enough to think he could cover it up with lies and deceit so that no one would ever know. But David was fortunate enough to have a trusted friend who refused to simply back off and pretend it didn't happen. Nathan cared enough to stand up and confront the king, who was on a collision course with exposure and defeat. He stood up courageously, in confidence and with love. David came clean. It hurt, but it also healed.

The sad truth in many relationships today is that too many simply cut what they could have untied. Some are quick to *criticize* instead of confront. Others seem to find joy in *condemning.* Then there are those who only want to *castigate.* Still others are quick to give their own self-righteous *counsel.* And, finally, some find it more convenient to simply *cancel* out of the relationship altogether. This is not how God wants His people to stand up for what is right.

Consider the apostle Paul's teachings. In Galatians 6:1–2, he called on us to "restore" the one who was in the wrong. The Greek word he chose, which we translate "restore" in our English Bibles, is actually a medical term. It was used to describe a physician who sees a man with a broken bone in his arm, and he puts it back into place so that it can mend and be useful again. Only God, the Great Physician, can truly heal relationships that need to be mended, but it is our job to get the bones properly aligned so that He can do His healing work. This, like the work of the physician, is often painful, but it is also necessary.

When we continuously back off and do not stand up, our conflicts tend to fester like an untreated boil that needs to be lanced or like a broken bone that is not properly set in place. While we may be trying to avoid pain, a refusal to stand up to wrong can actually result in even more pain and agitation in our relationships. On the other hand, we all have witnessed unresolved conflicts that are the result of someone standing up (often in anger), without first backing off to listen to his or her heart. In conflict resolution it is never a matter of "either . . . or," rather it is "both . . . and." There is definitely a time to stand up, but Nehemiah's example demonstrates that it should only come after a time of backing off. Rebuilders never cut what they can untie because they are convinced . . . *it's never too late for a new beginning!*

21 THERE IS A TIME TO GIVE IN

"I also, with my brethren and my servants, am lending them money and grain. Please, let us stop this usury! Restore now to them, even this day, their lands, their vineyards, their olive groves, and their houses, also a hundredth of the money and the grain, the new wine and the oil, that you have charged them."
—NEHEMIAH 5:10–11

*I*n successful conflict resolution, the time to back off and the time to stand up should always be followed by a time to give in. In verses 10–11 of chapter 5, Nehemiah challenged his Jewish brothers. If we listen closely enough, we can hear the conciliatory tone in his words, "I also, with my brethren and my servants, am lending them money and grain. Please, let us stop this usury! Restore now to them, even this day, their lands, their vineyards, their olive groves, and their houses, also a hundredth of the money and the grain, the new wine and the oil, that you have charged them" (Nehemiah 5:10–11). Nehemiah was saying to the nobles and ruler, "It is time to give in. See I am making this right too." He identified with his people, demonstrating that he was willing to follow through with the same actions he requested of them. He had stood up; now it was time to give in.

Nehemiah was not showing weakness here. Just the opposite. He was showing true strength. In fact, it takes more strength and security to give in than it does to stand up. Almost anyone can stand up. But those who resolve conflicts know there is also a time to give in on certain issues for the greater good. We must allow others to save face in the process of conflict resolution. There are times when giving in on nonessentials is the best policy. It is always best to lose a few little battles in order to win the larger war.

> There are times when giving in on nonessentials is the best policy. It is always best to lose a few little battles in order to win the larger war.

We see this exact principle practiced in the early church. When conflict arose and threatened the heart of unity of the new movement, the church leaders were wise enough to know that it was time to give in. Thousands of Jews from all over the Mediterranean world had flocked to Jerusalem for the Holy Days, which culminated in the Passover. While they were in the city, God's Spirit fell upon them on the day of Pentecost. In the aftermath, multitudes of these Hellenistic, Greek-speaking Jews, who had come to Jerusalem from far and wide, came to faith in Christ. They didn't return to their home countries, but remained in the city instead. At the same time, thousands of the Jews who lived there—the Hebraic, Hebrew-speaking Jews—also put their faith in the Messiah. The leaders of this early church, Peter and James, came from the Hebraic strain. Conflict arose when the Hellenistic Jews believed that they and those in need among them were being slighted by the church leaders who (they believed) were playing favorites with their own Hebraic brothers and sisters. At this point, Peter did an incredible thing to resolve the conflict. He appointed seven deacons to oversee the distribution of aid. But note this important fact: all seven of the men listed in Acts chapter 6, had Hellenistic names, meaning they all came from the very group who had raised the issue. Peter gave in. It was a beautiful display of conflict resolution. Skillfully, delicately, and with great determination, he untied the knot of the problem. Peter didn't cut what he could untie. He had a much larger war he wanted to win. The conflict was resolved, and the gospel continued to spread.

Returning to Nehemiah, we find him doing what he had been doing ever since he arrived in Jerusalem, leading by example. One of the key characteristics of his success was that he never asked his people to do something that he did not do himself. If he called them to work diligently on the wall, he was right there with them. If he asked them to pray, he was the first one on his knees. If they needed to work overtime, he was the last to leave. He consistently led by example. Now he asked them to do the right thing for those among them who were less privileged. And once again, he was at the front of the line. Being an example ourselves is vital in conflict resolution, whether it is in the home, at the office, in the social arena, or wherever.

We get a glimpse of how Nehemiah incorporated the principle of giving in during conflict resolution when we read his words in Nehemiah 5:14–19:

> *Moreover, from the time that I was appointed to be their governor in the land of Judah, from the twentieth year until the thirty-second year of King Artaxerxes, twelve years, neither I nor my brothers ate the governor's provisions. But the former governors who were before me laid burdens on the people, and took from them bread and wine, besides forty shekels of silver. Yes, even their servants bore rule over the people, but I did not do so, because of the fear of God. Indeed, I also continued the work on this wall, and we did not buy any land. All my servants were gathered there for the work.*

And at my table were one hundred and fifty Jews and rulers, besides those who came to us from the nations around us. Now that which was prepared daily was one ox and six choice sheep. Also fowl were prepared for me, and once every ten days an abundance of all kinds of wine. Yet in spite of this I did not demand the governor's provisions, because the bondage was heavy on this people.

Remember me, my God, for good, according to all that I have done for this people.

Nehemiah knew that nothing was more important than seeing the wall rebuilt and the gates rehung. Therefore, he was wise enough to know there was a time to give in.

Let's apply this in the area of parenting our children. What is most important? Is it to be able to say you won every argument, that you kept them under your thumb? Or is it more important to see that young man or woman grow up with virtue and values, convictions and commitments? In raising children there are times when we, as parents, need to back off and listen to our hearts. There are times when we need to stand up and give proper discipline. But there are also times when it is best to give in, to learn the lesson of losing a few little battles that are really not all that important on the way to winning the larger war.

Giving in on nonessentials is not a sign of weakness. It actually signals a hidden strength that can become contagious. Too many conflicts are left unsolved because people insist they must win every argument. They have never learned the lesson of giving in.

Rebuilders never cut what they can untie. They know there is a time to back off. They know there is a time to stand up. And they also discover the liberating principle that there is a time to give in. And then they discover the truth that . . . *it's never too late for a new beginning!*

THERE IS A TIME TO REACH OUT

"*I also, with my brethren and my servants, am lending them money and grain. Please, let us stop this usury! Restore now to them, even this day, their lands, their vineyards, their olive groves, and their houses, also a hundredth of the money and the grain, the new wine and the oil, that you have charged them.*"

So they said, "We will restore it, and will require nothing from them; we will do as you say."

Then I called the priests, and required an oath from them that they would do according to this promise. Then I shook out the fold of my garment and said, "So may God shake out each man from his house, and from his property, who does not perform this promise. Even thus may he be shaken out and emptied."

And all the assembly said, "Amen!" and praised the LORD. Then the people did according to this promise."

—NEHEMIAH 5:10–13

*N*ehemiah was pleading. He was reaching out to his people. He was building bridges, not barriers, in order to resolve conflicts within their ranks. Building consensus among the people is a vital element of conflict resolution.

Notice that there was a sense of urgency in the tone of his voice: "Restore now . . . even this day!" (Nehemiah 5:11). This was not a matter that he wanted the people to go home and ponder. He was reaching out to them with compassion coupled with passion. "Now! Do the right thing right now! What are you waiting for?" Yes, Nehemiah had been conciliatory, though he had not compromised his position. And, yes, he had backed off for a time, but this was the time to ask the nobles and the elders to join him in doing what was right.

Nehemiah was following the very pattern Jesus would later prescribe as the formula for conflict resolution. Jesus instructed:

> If your brother sins against you, go and tell him his fault between you and him alone. If he hears you, you have gained your brother. But if he will not hear, take with you one or two more, that "by the mouth of two or three witnesses every word may be established." And if he refuses to hear them, tell it to the church. (Matthew 18:15–17)

This was exactly what Nehemiah was doing. First, he

confronted his offenders in private. He said, "I told them" (Nehemiah 5:7, author's paraphrase). When his personal and private appeals were not met with a positive response, he moved on to a more public approach, which eventually won the day (5:7–12).

And what was the result of Nehemiah's four-fold approach to conflict resolution—of backing off, standing up, giving in, and then reaching out? It was this: "And all the assembly said, 'Amen!' and praised the LORD. Then the people did according to this promise" (5:13). Shalom returned!

The best practical illustration of Nehemiah's approach to conflict resolution is found tucked away near the end of your New Testament, in one of the shortest books of the Bible, an ancient letter known by its recipient's name, Philemon. These twenty-five short verses reveal the great apostle Paul putting Nehemiah's principles into play. This little letter from Paul to Philemon tells the story of conflict, resentment, and eventual reconciliation. On a previous journey through the region of Colosse, Paul led a wealthy and powerful man of the city to faith in Christ. His name was Philemon, and he started a church, which met regularly in his own home. Philemon had a contractual worker—a bond servant—under his authority, by the name of Onesimus. But one day, Onesimus stole some of his master's money and headed out to the big city and the bright lights of Rome. Through an amazing series of events, he was arrested and put in prison. Meanwhile, Paul had been imprisoned in Rome for preaching the gospel, and the two inmates found themselves sharing the same prison cell. It didn't take long before Paul had converted this runaway, rip-off artist to faith. Onesimus' life was totally transformed and his first mission after being released from prison was to journey back to Colosse, find Philemon, make restitution for his wrong, and seek reconciliation. So Paul wrote a letter to Philemon encouraging him to receive Onesimus as he would Paul himself, "no longer as a slave but . . . a beloved brother" (v. 16).

This letter, preserved for all to read in the Bible, is a case study in the art of conflict resolution. Paul began by backing off. He reminded Philemon that he made "mention of [him] always in [his] prayers" (Philemon 4). Then, Paul stood up to confront any possible opposition: "If then you count me as a partner, receive [Onesimus] as you would me" (17). Next, Paul gave in. Listen as he continued his letter: "If he has wronged you or owes anything, put that on my account. . . . I will repay" (18–19). And finally, Paul reached out by saying, "Having confidence in your obedience, I write to you, knowing that you will do even more than I say" (Philemon 21). These four principles of conflict resolution work. They worked in Nehemiah's day. They worked in Paul's day. And they will work in our day. They will work at home. They will work at the office. They will work in the social arena. They will work anywhere, anytime they are put into practice.

The entire Bible is a textbook in the art of conflict resolution. Consider Joseph. If there were ever a dysfunctional family unit, his was it. Jealousy, lying, plotting, and deception ripped his family apart, and it remained divided for many years. Motivated by burning jealousy, Joseph's brothers sold him into slavery, and he eventually found himself in Egypt. Through a miraculous set of events, Joseph was elevated to a position the equivalent of today's prime minister over the most progressive nation in the world at that time. When famine hit Israel, Joseph's brothers were desperate, and so they came to Egypt to try to buy grain. In one of the most moving scenes in recorded history, Joseph revealed and then reconciled himself to his brothers, who had no clue of what had happened to him so many years before. How was Joseph able to do this? First, he backed off. Before he met his brothers, the Bible records he went into a room by himself and wept. He backed off. He listened to his heart. Then, he revealed himself to them. He stood up. He came to them, confronted them, and exclaimed, "I am Joseph your brother!" Next, he gave in and then reached out. Joseph went to his brothers. They fell into each other's arms in a warm embrace of love and forgiveness. Joseph was one who didn't cut what he could untie.

And what about Jesus Himself? On almost every page of the Gospels, we find Him dealing with conflict. In Mark's gospel alone, we find others in conflict with Him on twenty-six different occasions. There was conflict in His hometown of Nazareth. There was conflict with His family, who sought to distance themselves from Him. There was conflict with His friends. There was conflict with the religious Pharisees. There was conflict with the disciples. There was conflict with Simon Peter. Conflict seemed to swirl around Him everywhere His sandaled feet took Him along the dusty paths of Judea and the Galilee. The Bible is the continuous story of Jesus resolving conflicts with folks like you and me.

> The Bible is the continuous story of Jesus resolving conflicts with folks like you and me.

Nehemiah's formula for conflict resolution only works when all four elements are incorporated into the equation and in proper sequence. But when used out of order or in isolation, these steps can take a bad situation and make it much worse.

Some people attempt to resolve their conflicts by employing only the first step. They back off, but then there is nothing more. They never stand up. They never give in. They never reach out. They just back off, period, end of sentence. This could be called the "lose-lose" approach to relationships. For example, how many parents have found themselves caving when conflict arises with their own children? That is, they give in time and time again without ever standing up to their own kids—often with disastrous consequences. When we play the conflict resolution game like this, both "sides" lose in the process. If Nehemiah had only backed off, the wall never would have been completed. He would have lost. And everyone would have lost too.

Others play the conflict-resolution game by employing only the second step. They stand up. Every time. And that is all they do. They are right, and there is no room for argument. This is called the "win-lose" approach to conflict resolution, and it never succeeds. It is a dead-end street that goes nowhere. These people only have relationships if they win every single point and the other person always loses. Had Nehemiah played the game this way, the wall never would have been rebuilt.

Then, there are those who attempt conflict resolution by employing only the third step. They never back off. They never stand up. All they do is give in, time after time after time, always and in all ways. This can be called the "lose-win" approach to reconciliation. That is, some people have such a low sense of their own self-worth, that they think the only way anyone would relate to them is if they always put themselves down and place the other person high above them. These individuals never solve their conflicts because they forfeit any respect others might have for them.

There is a time to back off, stand up, give in, and there is also a time to reach out. When each of these four steps is practiced in the proper order, we learn—as Nehemiah learned—to solve our own conflicts. This is called the "win-win" approach.

Consider our own relationship with the Lord Jesus. You and I were in conflict with Him, with His purpose, and with His plan for our lives. We had a good start in a perfect paradise. But we chose to go our own way and do our own thing. Each of us. All of us: "for all have sinned and fall short of the glory of God" (Romans 3:23). So, what did the Lord do to resolve this conflict and bring us into a restored relationship with Him? First, Jesus backed off. In His darkest hour, He knelt beneath those gnarled, old olive trees in Gethsemane's garden. In "serious thought" He backed off and took counsel with His heart. Listen to

His impassioned plea: "Father, if it is Your will, take this cup away from Me; nevertheless not My will, but Yours, be done" (Luke 22:42). Jesus knew the first step in any conflict resolution was to back off.

Next, we watch as He stood up. And my, did He stand up! Before Caiaphas, the high priest. Before Herod, the puppet king. Before Pilate, the Roman procurator. Before all His accusers, Jesus stood up. When asked, "Are you then the Son of God?" He boldly replied, "You rightly say that I am" (Luke 22:70). Jesus stood up.

Then, Jesus gave in. Jesus had a goal in His mind, to rebuild the broken relationships between us and Him, between us and God. So He gave in. Don't let anyone tell you He was pushed and shoved and kicked up the Via Dolorosa that day on His way to Calvary's cross. He went "as a lamb to the slaughter" (Isaiah 53:7). Willingly, Jesus laid down His life. No one took it from Him. He gave in for you and for me.

And finally, Jesus reached out. Can you, in your mind's eye, see Him now? He is suspended between heaven and earth on a Roman cross outside the city wall of Jerusalem. His arms are outstretched in welcome. He is reaching out. Inviting. Imploring you and me to be "reconciled to God" (Romans 5:10).

Talk about conflict resolution. The Lord Jesus is the

epitome of it. In fact, He wrote the book on it—the Bible is the greatest, continuous story of conflict resolution ever written.

We don't have to keep journeying through life like that impatient, young boy who played with me on the old vacant lot. You don't have to wear "shoes" of reconciliation that lace only halfway to the top because you have cut off the knot. Rebuilders, like Nehemiah, know that. And they get it. That is why rebuilders never cut what they can untie. They are convinced . . . *it's never too late for a new beginning!*

PART 6

Rebuilders

Finish Strong

*T*wo of modern evangelicalism's most revered and respected men were the late Billy Graham and Chuck Colson. Billy Graham's entire life can be summed up with two words—character and integrity. After years in the public eye, and throughout his life, his character remained beyond reproach and his reputation spotless. He never got off on a side street or spent time on the sidelines. Conversely, however, Chuck Colson's life came crashing down like Jerusalem's wall. He wandered off down several side streets and found himself on the sidelines in a prison cell. But then he came back and rebuilt a life of character and conviction. He left a legacy through his ministry of Prison Fellowship that still exists as Christ's own hand extended, giving help and eternal hope to thousands of prisoners and their families. Colson and Graham have this in common—they both finished strong.

For decades, Billy Graham was one of the most recognized names in the entire English-speaking world. His preaching ministry burst onto the American scene while he was still a young man in the 1940s. However, he had two contemporaries, who, at the time, were much better known and promised to be much brighter stars on the national scene. But strangely, few people today have ever even heard of Chuck Templeton or Bron Clifford. In William Martin's biography of Billy Graham, he relates that Chuck Templeton was the most gifted and talented young preacher of his era.

Billy Graham, Chuck Templeton, and Bron Clifford were all greatly sought-after young preachers. In 1946, the National Association of Evangelicals published an article entitled, "The Best Used Men of God." That article highlighted the ministry of Chuck Templeton, but made no mention of Billy Graham. Today, we have heard of Billy Graham, but whatever happened to Chuck Templeton and Bron Clifford?

Bron Clifford started out in the ministry at a young age. When he was only twenty-five, he was already preaching to massive crowds that numbered in the thousands. Met by overflow crowds everywhere he went, it was said that he had touched more lives and broke more attendance records than any evangelist in American history. He was tall and handsome, intelligent and eloquent. He soon caught the attention of Hollywood producers seeking to entice him to play significant roles in movies. That turned out to be a disastrous side street for him. By the mid-1950s, Clifford had lost his health and his family, and he was plagued by alcoholism. At the age of thirty-five, this great preacher died alone in a rundown motel room on the outskirts of Amarillo, Texas. Chuck Templeton also left the ministry, but to pursue a career in journalism. Sadly, by the early 1950s, this once-gifted preacher of the gospel was reported to no longer believe in Christ in the orthodox sense.

> No matter how gifted one may or may not be, rebuilders have at least one characteristic in common: they finish strong.

The moral? No matter how gifted one may or may not be, rebuilders have at least one characteristic in common: they finish strong. They don't detour off onto side streets or allow themselves to be relegated to the sidelines.

Chuck Colson, however, was the epitome of a rebuilder. Caught up in the cover-up of his own Watergate crimes, his walls collapsed and his gates burned down. He detoured off onto side streets and was relegated to the sidelines of prison. But he didn't stay there; he came back. Even today, years after his death, his presence is felt in Prison Fellowship gatherings around the world, giving hope and help to thousands who are also battling to rebuild their lives.

As we come now to the sixth chapter of Nehemiah, many of us, like him, are seeking to rebuild something that has been broken. It has been a long journey for Nehemiah— from Persia, where he first heard the report of Jerusalem's broken wall, to his leaving the comforts and security of his life as the king's cupbearer, to becoming the rebuilder of the broken wall of Jerusalem. Much has changed since he made that solitary midnight ride to review the ruins. The wall was up, and Nehemiah had the finish line in sight. All that remained was to hang the gates (Nehemiah 6:1).

At last, the goal was in sight. The finish line. "Mission Accomplished" just ahead. But be warned: this is the most dangerous point in any rebuilding process. This is when the enemy comes along with one final attempt to divert us from our goal. The enemy first tried to detour Nehemiah onto a side street. But Nehemiah kept his focus and replied to that temptation with a question: "Why should the work cease while I leave it and go down to you?" (6:3). So then his enemies tried to relegate Nehemiah to the sidelines. But he remained faithful and fired off another question instead: "Should such a man as I flee?" (6:11).

Of all the wonderful things one could say about Nehemiah, the best is this: he finished strong. And, before he steps off the scene of Scripture, he leaves us with a valuable lesson on how we can do the same. It is not so much how long our personal race may be, nor even how difficult the obstacles we face along the way, but it is how we finish that matters most.

Seeing the finish line ahead, Nehemiah sprinted toward the tape while shouting two important principles to us that keep echoing down through the corridors of the centuries: "Stay off the side streets. Keep focused! Stay off the sidelines. Keep faithful!" He wanted to ensure that it might be said of you and me, "So the wall was finished" (6:15). After all . . . *it's never too late for a new beginning!*

23 STAY OFF THE SIDE STREETS: KEEP FOCUSED

Now it happened when Sanballat, Tobiah, Geshem the Arab, and the rest of our enemies heard that I had rebuilt the wall, and that there were no breaks left in it (though at that time I had not hung the doors in the gates), that Sanballat and Geshem sent to me, saying, "Come, let us meet together among the villages in the plain of Ono." But they thought to do me harm.

So I sent messengers to them, saying, "I am doing a great work, so that I cannot come down. Why should the work cease while I leave it and go down to you?"

But they sent me this message four times, and I answered them in the same manner.

Then Sanballat sent his servant to me as before, the fifth time, with an open letter in his hand. In it was written:

> *It is reported among the nations, and Geshem says, that you and the Jews plan to rebel; therefore, according to these rumors, you are rebuilding the wall, that you may be their king. And you have also appointed prophets to proclaim concerning you at Jerusalem, saying, "There is a king in Judah!" Now these matters will be reported*

to the king. So come, therefore, and let us consult together.

Then I sent to him, saying, "No such things as you say are being done, but you invent them in your own heart."

For they all were trying to make us afraid, saying, "Their hands will be weakened in the work, and it will not be done."

Now therefore, O God, strengthen my hands.

—NEHEMIAH 6:1–9

Our family spent fifteen wonderful years living in Fort Lauderdale, Florida, known as the "Venice of America" due to its almost two hundred miles of waterways inside the city limits. There are thousands of homes located on man-made canals that wind their way through the city. Water taxis are a popular means of transportation. Street after street dead-ends into one of those canals. It took me a while to learn that if I were going to get anywhere in the city, I needed to stay on the main roads. Each time I thought I could beat the traffic by getting off on a side street, I would find myself staring into the dead end of a canal. This is a good lesson for all rebuilders. Staying off the side streets and keeping our focus is crucial if we want to reach our final destination.

As Nehemiah's story unfolds, his old nemesis,

Sanballat, along with his deceitful allies, reappear on the scene. Hearing that Nehemiah had finished rebuilding the wall and all that was left to do was hang the gates, these enemies made one final attempt to derail him. "Come, let us meet . . . in the plain of Ono," they requested (Nehemiah 6:2). They appeared to be offering to meet him halfway. But they were really seeking to trap him at his own game of conflict resolution. By challenging him to sit down with them in the Plain of Ono, they were saying, "Come on, Nehemiah, and practice what you have just preached. Give in and reach out." But Nehemiah was wise enough to know this was not a time to give in; instead, it was a time to stand up, stay off the side streets, and finish the wall. Thus, when they invited him to come to the Plain of Ono, his reply was "No!"—not just once, but four separate times.

Often, when our wall is virtually complete and our task is almost done, we are tempted to think we are safely in the home stretch. Then some Sanballat comes along and tries to lure us onto a side street at our own Plain of Ono. Notice that Nehemiah's response to his tempters came in the form a question: "I am doing a great work. . . . Why should the work cease while I leave it and go down to you?" (6:3). Despite this answer, Nehemiah's enemies persisted: "They sent me this message four times, and I answered them in the same manner" (6:4). Your enemies will persist too. But remember Nehemiah and keep answering them "in the same manner."

Next, Nehemiah's enemies sent an open letter stating, "It is reported among the nations, and Geshem says, that you and the Jews plan to rebel; therefore, according to these rumors, you are rebuilding the wall, that you may be their king" (6:6). Note the words, "It is reported among the nations." Rumors generally have two distinguishing characteristics: they are nameless and shameless. Have you ever noticed how the sources of rumors are seldom ever mentioned? Why? Because most of the time they prefer to remain nameless. Rumors are also shameless—that is, they are often exaggerated or just outright lies. In this case, Nehemiah's enemies lied with a baseless assertion that his real motive was to be king of Judah. This letter was nothing more than an attempt to divert Nehemiah's focus and get him off on a side street before his task was completed. But one of his greatest strengths was his laser-like focus.

As we tackle our own rebuilding projects, we, too, may become the target of a shameless rumor. We would do well to deal with them in the same way Nehemiah did. Consider his words: "No such things as you say are being done, but you invent them in your own heart. . . . Now therefore, O God, strengthen my hands" (6:8–9). Rumors should be dealt with in three distinct ways. *Refute them. Rebuke them. Refer them.* First, Nehemiah refuted the rumors about him: "No such things as you say are being done." Next, he rebuked them saying, "You invent them in your own heart." Then he simply referred to the Lord and left those rumors there: "Now, therefore, O God, strengthen my hands." This is good advice for any of us who may be the victim of rumors while in the rebuilding process. Refute them, rebuke them, and then refer to the Lord.

The Plain of Ono was nothing more than a side street. There may have been nothing inherently wrong with it. But it was a potentially disastrous side street for Nehemiah. And, chances are, at one time or another, we will all find ourselves distracted by a side street. When our children were young, we always looked at family vacations as investing in life memories with our family. One summer, we took a car trip from Fort Lauderdale to our nation's capital, Washington, DC. Because it is hundreds of miles from south Florida to the Georgia border, it took us more than a day just to get out of Florida. On the second day, we found ourselves winding our way through the mountains of North Carolina and Virginia. I noted on the map a certain road that appeared to be a wonderful shortcut, shaving off scores of miles to our destination. So we took that side road. What I did not know was that it was mile after mile of a winding, mountainous, two-lane road, filled with hundreds of large trucks. What I thought was going to be a shortcut ended up adding hours to our trip, not to mention the interesting exchanges taking place in the front seat of our car! Life is like that, isn't it? It is filled with side streets that look so inviting, but end up being paved with frustration and, too often, leading to failure.

It is possible to do everything right, and then allow ourselves to be pulled off onto a side street just before our task is finished. I have seen this happen in marriages. It can happen in other relationships. It shows up in business. There will always be a Sanballat trying to get us off the main road.

Listen to Nehemiah's response to his enemies: "I am doing a great work, so that I cannot come down. Why should the work cease while I leave it and go down to you?" (6:3). Nehemiah saw his task as "a great work." Rebuilding *is* a great work. This is especially true when we have the finish line in sight. Little trips down to the Plain of Ono delay or destroy our "great work." And it's important to note that many side streets are not marked with flashing Danger or Dead End signs. In fact, side streets are not always inherently bad. They may even be good things, just not the best thing. And remember: good is always the enemy of the best. Stay focused.

Perhaps that wall you have been rebuilding is up at last, and all that remains is to hang your gates. Just remember, in rebuilding, getting near the finish line is the most dangerous time in the entire journey. Therefore, give heed to Nehemiah's good advice: "Stay off the side streets. Keep focused." Because you, too, are doing a great work and cannot come down. Rebuilders finish strong because they have known all along . . . *it's never too late for a new beginning!*

24 STAY OFF THE SIDELINES: KEEP FAITHFUL

Afterward I came to the house of Shemaiah the son of Delaiah, the son of Mehetabel, who was a secret informer; and he said, "Let us meet together in the house of God, within the temple, and let us close the doors of the temple, for they are coming to kill you; indeed, at night they will come to kill you."

And I said, "Should such a man as I flee? And who is there such as I who would go into the temple to save his life? I will not go in!" Then I perceived that God had not sent him at all, but that he pronounced this prophecy against me because Tobiah and Sanballat had hired him. For this reason he was hired, that I should be afraid and act that way and sin, so that they might have cause for an evil report, that they might reproach me.

My God, remember Tobiah and Sanballat, according to these their works, and the prophetess Noadiah and the rest of the prophets who would have made me afraid.

So the wall was finished on the twenty-fifth day of Elul, in fifty-two days. And it happened, when all our enemies heard of it, and all the nations around us saw these things, that they

were very disheartened in their own eyes; for they perceived
that this work was done by our God.

—NEHEMIAH 6:10–16

*A*nyone who has ever played on an athletic team
does not like to be on the sidelines when the game
is being played. Anyone aspiring to be an actor takes no
joy in standing backstage in the wings when all the action
is taking place on center stage. Rebuilders finish strong
because they resist the temptation to get off on side streets,
and because they stay in the game and off the sidelines by
keeping focused and faithful.

Some would say my own athletic career reached its
apex when I was selected to the all-star team decades ago
in the East Side Little League in Fort Worth. We played
our games at the old Del Murray Field, and I played for the
Rox Ex Exterminating Company Tigers. I can still feel the
weight of those old gray flannel uniforms with the orange
trim. My Little League coach was a man by the name of
Jerry Peden. He was a big guy, especially in the eyes of a
ten-year-old like me, playing on a team of mostly eleven-
and twelve-year-olds. At every practice, Mr. Peden would
drill into our young minds these words: "Don't get called
out on strikes." He wanted to make sure that if we were
going to strike out, then we would go down swinging at

the pitch and not standing there with the bat on our shoulders. Whenever I would be at bat and get two strikes, I would look down the third base line where Mr. Peden was standing in the coach's box. He would stare at me, cup his hands to his mouth, and shout those words, "Don't get called out on strikes." Even as I type this, I can still sense the fear I felt when I heard those words.

Nehemiah has been overcoming all sorts of obstacles in his rebuilding project. There came opposition from without—strike one. There was opposition from within—strike two. Now, just before he hits a home run by finishing his task, the enemy throws him a curveball: "Let us meet together in the house of God, within the temple" (Nehemiah 6:10). Had he done so, Nehemiah would have been placed on the sidelines for the rest of his life, which might not have been very much longer. But he was too wise to get called out on strikes. Nehemiah was not only focused; he stayed faithful.

It is one thing to get off on a side street, but it is something altogether different to be put on the sidelines and out of the game. When Nehemiah's enemies sought to lure him into a meeting with them "within the temple," this was definitely an attempt to put

> It is one thing to get off on a side street, but it is something altogether different to be put on the sidelines and out of the game.

him out of the game. To meet "within the temple" meant to go into the inner sanctum of the Holy Place where only the priest was allowed to enter. King Uzziah found out the hard way that this was a terrible idea in 2 Chronicles 26. He was fortunate to escape with his life, but this infringement on God's instruction cost him his health and left him with a life of leprosy. So this call to meet "within the temple" was a blatant attempt to put Nehemiah on the sidelines before the rebuilding was complete.

But Nehemiah was faithful, and so he recognized the trap. He was a man who lived his life under the authority of God's Word. He submitted to the God of the Word and the Word of God.

As when he was tempted to get off on a side street, Nehemiah once again answered with a question, "Should such a man as I flee?" (Nehemiah 6:11). If the Plain of Ono was a side street, going "within the temple" would mean being taken out of the game and placed on the sidelines. Our own experiences are replete with men and women we have known who got started right, but who—when the end was in sight—were unfaithful, made wrong decisions, and ended up on the sidelines. Too many of my own peers in ministry got off on all kinds of side streets, lost their focus and faithfulness, and ended up on the sidelines, out of the game.

Nehemiah's question was rhetorical. He had no intention of fleeing. Too many people today are fleeing, running away from life and opportunities. Escapism takes all kinds of forms. Some who have spent so much time rebuilding relationships end up fleeing them before the job is completed. Some invest years, even decades, in marriages only to flee before the finish line.

The psalmist feared this. He said, "Oh, that I had wings like a dove! I would fly away and be at rest" (Psalm 55:6). A lot of us can echo that same sentiment. But it is time for a reality check. You don't have any wings! You can't fly off. You can't run out on life every time things are not going your way.

How we finish our race is what ultimately matters most. Consider Nehemiah's finish: "So the wall was finished" (Nehemiah 6:15). This is the biggest understatement in Nehemiah's entire record. But we would never have read those words if Nehemiah had not run his race the way he did. We should all allow Nehemiah's question to be branded into our own thinking process: "Should such a man as I flee?" And we, like Nehemiah, should answer with a resounding, "No! Never!"

Notice that when the wall was completed, there came an interesting aftermath. "And it happened, when all our enemies heard of it, and all the nations around us saw these things, that they were very disheartened in their own eyes; for they perceived that this work was done by our God" (6:16). God did it, and Nehemiah gave Him the glory for it. There are some who trust God while climbing the ladder to success, but then they soon forget Him when they reach the top. Not Nehemiah. And neither should we.

Rebuilders finish strong. Always. In every area of life. Think about the following examples:

- Who generally wins a professional golf tournament? The one who finishes the strongest. Even though the tournament consists of seventy-two holes played over four days, it is the golfer who plays every hole—especially the final two or three—with focus and passion who wins. He or she may even have hit the ball out of bounds on a previous round, but that golfer knows it's possible to finish strong and still win. Because it is never too late for a new beginning.

- The same is true in basketball. One of the greatest spectator events of the year is the annual "Final Four" college basketball tournament. The team that plays the best in the final two minutes of each tournament game, who finishes strongest, is the most likely to win the championship. Maybe you fouled out in a previous game. Maybe you didn't make a single shot. So what? Get up. Get off the sidelines. Get back in the game. Keep focused and faithful. There is still time for the wall to be completed.

- In the Olympic Games, the mile run is one of the signature events. Even though those runners have been running around the track for almost a mile, the outcome generally comes down to the final fifty yards of the race. The one who finishes the strongest is the one who gets the medal.

- My daughter is an attorney and has spent much of her time in the courtroom, arguing various litigation cases. Jury selection is an important part of winning a trial. Opening arguments are vital in setting the direction of the case. The examination and the cross-examination of witnesses are crucial. But it is that final argument given to the jury that leaves the lasting impression. Usually, the attorney who finishes the case the strongest is the one who wins the verdict.

If this fact is true in golf, basketball, track, and even in the courtroom, it is most definitely also true in rebuilding our lives. Whether we are rebuilding a home, a relationship, a marriage, a vocation, a business, a church, or anything else, those who get the job completed have at least this one characteristic in common: they finish strong.

We will be remembered by how we finish our race. I have a world of admiration for the men and women I have known in life who, for a while, might have lost focus or even faithfulness, but who then battled back to finish strong. Some had gotten off on a side street. Others were put on the sideline. Yet they got up and got back in the race. Some might be running with a slight limp, but they are back running their race and seeking to finish strong. Some of us, in a weak moment, may have gone down to the Plain of Ono and met the enemy halfway. But it is never too late to get back in the race.

The thing that really matters for each of us is seeing our wall finished. The gospel of Mark in our New Testament is one of my favorite books. It was actually written by a man named John Mark who is the epitome of what Nehemiah taught about finishing strong. Do you remember him? He started out right. He was one of Paul's prize students. He even journeyed with Paul on that first missionary journey. But then he quit. He lost his focus and got off on a side street. He left the great apostle in a lurch. Later, however, encouraged by Barnabas, John Mark got up, got back in the race, and finished strong. He was even commended by Paul, himself, in one of his final epistles. We all need a Barnabas in our lives to encourage us. And we all need to be a Barnabas to someone else. Every time I read the gospel of Mark, I am reminded that it is never too late for a new beginning.

And no one ever finished a race stronger than the Lord Jesus Christ. The devil sought to get Him on a side street. He took Him to a high mountain and tempted Him to bow down. When that failed, Satan took our Savior to the pinnacle of the temple to appeal to His pride, inviting Him to jump and prove His deity. But Jesus kept focused on God's Word. Finally, the enemy sought to put Him on the sidelines. The crowds jeered, mocked, spat in His face, ridiculed, and screamed, "If You are the Son of God, come down from the cross" (Matthew 27:40). In that very moment, Jesus could have called an army of thousands of angelic hosts to set Him free. But He was finishing strong, as if echoing Nehemiah's own words, "I am doing a great work, so that I cannot come down. Why should the work cease while I leave it and go down to you?" (Nehemiah 6:3). Our Lord kept focused, and He kept faithful. He finished strong. And in the end, on the cross, He said, "It is finished!" (John 19:30). And to prove it, three days later, He arose from the grave, the ever-living Lord and Savior.

I don't know about you, but I know about me. I want to finish strong. I want to stay off the side streets and keep focused. I want to stay off the sidelines and keep faithful. Our Lord stands at the finish line, waiting for each of us. His arms are still outstretched in welcome. He is more interested in your rebuilding project than you are. He believes in you. It is time for you to believe in Him. Rebuilders all finish strong, and in doing so, they prove . . . *it's never too late for a new beginning!*

EPILOGUE

*W*e are all different in many and varied ways. But we all have one thing in common: not a single one of us is perfect. We are all in need of rebuilding from within. When it comes to a personal knowledge and faith in the Lord Jesus Christ, all of us need to get started right on this journey. So let's begin as Nehemiah did.

Make an honest evaluation of your situation. The Bible says we "all have sinned and fall short of the glory of God" (Romans 3:23). We humans had a really good start. Life began wonderfully for us in Eden's garden. The climate was never too warm and never too cold. We never had an ache or a single pain. There were no worries, no heartaches. God had placed us in a perfect paradise. But then Satan came around, cast a seed of doubt into our hearts, and we fell into sin (Genesis 3). And we have been on a personal journey of trying to get back home—back into God's presence—ever since. We each begin our own inner rebuilding process when we make an honest evaluation of ourselves, confessing that we have missed the mark and gone our own way.

Identify the need. There is a God-shaped vacuum in every human heart, a void that only He can fill. Oh, we stay busy trying to fill it with all kinds of other things or people, but it never works. Fortunately, we have a Savior, Jesus, who loves us so much that He clothed Himself in human flesh and walked among us to identify with our own need. He took your sin in Himself as He hung on the cross, dying your death so that you could live His life, taking your sin so you could take His righteousness. The *something* you have been searching for all your life is really *Someone*, whose sweet name is Jesus.

Take personal responsibility. Our sin is not some little vice we can laugh off. It is so serious that it necessitated the cross. It is not to be excused just because everyone else is doing it. It is not to be minimized because it is not as bad as someone else's. We must take personal responsibility for our sin and acknowledge the gospel, the good news that Jesus died in our place to make a way out of what seemed to be inescapable for us. He was buried, and He rose again on the third day, our ever-living Lord and Savior, defeating both sin and death. Taking personal responsibility means admitting that you are a sinner and putting your faith in Him and in Him alone.

Move out of your comfort zone. Finally, a personal faith means that you transfer your trust in yourself over to trust in Christ alone for your salvation. Jesus said, "Behold, I stand at the door and knock. If anyone hears My voice and opens the door, I will come in to him" (Revelation 3:20). There is, in fact, a door to your heart, and Jesus is knocking on it right now. And if you are willing to move out of your comfort zone, you can respond to Him right now. He has promised that "whoever calls on the name of the LORD shall be saved" (Romans 10:13). If this reflects the desire of your heart, then you can pray this prayer right now:

Dear Lord Jesus, I know I have sinned and am undeserving of eternal life with You. Please forgive me. Thank You for taking my sin on the cross and dying in my place, dying the very death I deserve. You are the only hope of eternal salvation. I ask You right now to be the Lord and King of my life. My heart's desire is for a new beginning with You. I turn my face to You, accepting Your gracious gift of forgiveness and eternal life. Thank You, Lord, for coming into my life and becoming my personal Lord and Savior. In Jesus' name, amen.

A simple prayer can never save you, but Jesus can and will! If this prayer expresses the desire of your heart, you can claim—as your very own—the promise Jesus made to all who would choose to follow Him: "Most assuredly, . . . he who believes in Me has everlasting life" (John 6:47).

Now that you have gotten started right on your own spiritual journey, you are ready for the great adventure for which Christ created you in the first place: to know your Lord in the intimacy of Father and child, and to walk with Him daily from this day forward. Follow Nehemiah's example as you travel along your own journey by finishing strong. Stay off the side streets. Keep focused. Stay off the sidelines. Keep faithful.

As we leave our friend Nehemiah, and the many truths he has given us, we can now testify ourselves to the beautiful reality . . . *it's never too late for a new beginning!*

APPENDIX
Nehemiah 1–6

NEHEMIAH PRAYS FOR HIS PEOPLE

1 The words of Nehemiah the son of Hachaliah.

It came to pass in the month of Chislev, in the twentieth year, as I was in Shushan the citadel, ² that Hanani one of my brethren came with men from Judah; and I asked them concerning the Jews who had escaped, who had survived the captivity, and concerning Jerusalem. ³ And they said to me, "The survivors who are left from the captivity in the province are there in great distress and reproach. The wall of Jerusalem is also broken down, and its gates are burned with fire."

⁴ So it was, when I heard these words, that I sat down and wept, and mourned for many days; I was fasting and praying before the God of heaven.

⁵ And I said: "I pray, LORD God of heaven, O great and awesome God, You who keep Your covenant and mercy with those who love You and observe Your commandments, ⁶ please let Your ear be attentive and Your eyes open, that You may hear the prayer of Your servant which I pray before You now, day and night, for the children of Israel Your servants, and confess the sins of the children of Israel which we have sinned against You. Both my father's house and I have sinned. ⁷ We have acted very corruptly against You, and have not kept the commandments, the statutes, nor the ordinances which You commanded Your servant Moses. ⁸ Remember, I pray, the word that You commanded Your servant Moses, saying, 'If you are unfaithful, I will scatter you among the nations; ⁹ but if

you return to Me, and keep My commandments and do them, though some of you were cast out to the farthest part of the heavens, yet I will gather them from there, and bring them to the place which I have chosen as a dwelling for My name.' ¹⁰ Now these are Your servants and Your people, whom You have redeemed by Your great power, and by Your strong hand. ¹¹ O Lord, I pray, please let Your ear be attentive to the prayer of Your servant, and to the prayer of Your servants who desire to fear Your name; and let Your servant prosper this day, I pray, and grant him mercy in the sight of this man."

For I was the king's cupbearer.

NEHEMIAH SENT TO JUDAH

2 And it came to pass in the month of Nisan, in the twentieth year of King Artaxerxes, when wine was before him, that I took the wine and gave it to the king. Now I had never been sad in his presence before. ² Therefore the king said to me, "Why is your face sad, since you are not sick? This is nothing but sorrow of heart."

So I became dreadfully afraid, ³ and said to the king, "May the king live forever! Why should my face not be sad, when the city, the place of my fathers' tombs, lies waste, and its gates are burned with fire?"

⁴ Then the king said to me, "What do you request?"

So I prayed to the God of heaven. ⁵ And I said to the king, "If it pleases the king, and if your servant has found favor in your sight, I ask that you send me to Judah, to the city of my fathers' tombs, that I may rebuild it."

⁶ Then the king said to me (the queen also sitting beside him), "How long will your journey be? And when will you return?" So it pleased the king to send me; and I set him a time.

⁷ Furthermore I said to the king, "If it pleases the king, let letters be given to me for the governors of the region beyond the River, that they must permit me to pass through till I come to Judah, ⁸ and a letter to Asaph the keeper of the

king's forest, that he must give me timber to make beams for the gates of the citadel which pertains to the temple, for the city wall, and for the house that I will occupy." And the king granted them to me according to the good hand of my God upon me.

9 Then I went to the governors in the region beyond the River, and gave them the king's letters. Now the king had sent captains of the army and horsemen with me. 10 When Sanballat the Horonite and Tobiah the Ammonite official heard of it, they were deeply disturbed that a man had come to seek the well-being of the children of Israel.

NEHEMIAH VIEWS THE WALL OF JERUSALEM

11 So I came to Jerusalem and was there three days. 12 Then I arose in the night, I and a few men with me; I told no one what my God had put in my heart to do at Jerusalem; nor was there any animal with me, except the one on which I rode. 13 And I went out by night through the Valley Gate to the Serpent Well and the Refuse Gate, and viewed the walls of Jerusalem which were broken down and its gates which were burned with fire. 14 Then I went on to the Fountain Gate and to the King's Pool, but there was no room for the animal under me to pass. 15 So I went up in the night by the valley, and viewed the wall; then I turned back and entered by the Valley Gate, and so returned. 16 And the officials did not know where I had gone or what I had done; I had not yet told the Jews, the priests, the nobles, the officials, or the others who did the work.

17 Then I said to them, "You see the distress that we are in, how Jerusalem lies waste, and its gates are burned with fire. Come and let us build the wall of Jerusalem, that we may no longer be a reproach." 18 And I told them of the hand of my God which had been good upon me, and also of the king's words that he had spoken to me.

So they said, "Let us rise up and build." Then they set their hands to this good work.

¹⁹ But when Sanballat the Horonite, Tobiah the Ammonite official, and Geshem the Arab heard of it, they laughed at us and despised us, and said, "What is this thing that you are doing? Will you rebel against the king?"

²⁰ So I answered them, and said to them, "The God of heaven Himself will prosper us; therefore we His servants will arise and build, but you have no heritage or right or memorial in Jerusalem."

REBUILDING THE WALL

3 Then Eliashib the high priest rose up with his brethren the priests and built the Sheep Gate; they consecrated it and hung its doors. They built as far as the Tower of the Hundred, and consecrated it, then as far as the Tower of Hananel. ² Next to Eliashib the men of Jericho built. And next to them Zaccur the son of Imri built.

³ Also the sons of Hassenaah built the Fish Gate; they laid its beams and hung its doors with its bolts and bars. ⁴ And next to them Meremoth the son of Urijah, the son of Koz, made repairs. Next to them Meshullam the son of Berechiah, the son of Meshezabel, made repairs. Next to them Zadok the son of Baana made repairs. ⁵ Next to them the Tekoites made repairs; but their nobles did not put their shoulders to the work of their Lord.

⁶ Moreover Jehoiada the son of Paseah and Meshullam the son of Besodeiah repaired the Old Gate; they laid its beams and hung its doors, with its bolts and bars. ⁷ And next to them Melatiah the Gibeonite, Jadon the Meronothite, the men of Gibeon and Mizpah, repaired the residence of the governor of the region beyond the River. ⁸ Next to him Uzziel the son of Harhaiah, one of the goldsmiths, made repairs. Also next to him Hananiah, one of the perfumers, made repairs; and they fortified Jerusalem as far as the Broad Wall. ⁹ And next to them Rephaiah the son of Hur, leader of half the district of Jerusalem, made repairs. ¹⁰ Next to them Jedaiah the son of Harumaph made repairs in

front of his house. And next to him Hattush the son of Hashabniah made repairs.

¹¹ Malchijah the son of Harim and Hashub the son of Pahath-Moab repaired another section, as well as the Tower of the Ovens. ¹² And next to him was Shallum the son of Hallohesh, leader of half the district of Jerusalem; he and his daughters made repairs.

¹³ Hanun and the inhabitants of Zanoah repaired the Valley Gate. They built it, hung its doors with its bolts and bars, and repaired a thousand cubits of the wall as far as the Refuse Gate.

¹⁴ Malchijah the son of Rechab, leader of the district of Beth Haccerem, repaired the Refuse Gate; he built it and hung its doors with its bolts and bars.

¹⁵ Shallun the son of Col-Hozeh, leader of the district of Mizpah, repaired the Fountain Gate; he built it, covered it, hung its doors with its bolts and bars, and repaired the wall of the Pool of Shelah by the King's Garden, as far as the stairs that go down from the City of David. ¹⁶ After him Nehemiah the son of Azbuk, leader of half the district of Beth Zur, made repairs as far as the place in front of the tombs of David, to the man-made pool, and as far as the House of the Mighty.

¹⁷ After him the Levites, under Rehum the son of Bani, made repairs. Next to him Hashabiah, leader of half the district of Keilah, made repairs for his district. ¹⁸ After him their brethren, under Bavai the son of Henadad, leader of the other half of the district of Keilah, made repairs. ¹⁹ And next to him Ezer the son of Jeshua, the leader of Mizpah, repaired another section in front of the Ascent to the Armory at the buttress. ²⁰ After him Baruch the son of Zabbai carefully repaired the other section, from the buttress to the door of the house of Eliashib the high priest. ²¹ After him Meremoth the son of Urijah, the son of Koz, repaired another section, from the door of the house of Eliashib to the end of the house of Eliashib.

²² And after him the

priests, the men of the plain, made repairs. ²³ After him Benjamin and Hasshub made repairs opposite their house. After them Azariah the son of Maaseiah, the son of Ananiah, made repairs by his house. ²⁴ After him Binnui the son of Henadad repaired another section, from the house of Azariah to the buttress, even as far as the corner. ²⁵ Palal the son of Uzai made repairs opposite the buttress, and on the tower which projects from the king's upper house that was by the court of the prison. After him Pedaiah the son of Parosh made repairs.

²⁶ Moreover the Nethinim who dwelt in Ophel made repairs as far as the place in front of the Water Gate toward the east, and on the projecting tower. ²⁷ After them the Tekoites repaired another section, next to the great projecting tower, and as far as the wall of Ophel.

²⁸ Beyond the Horse Gate the priests made repairs, each in front of his own house. ²⁹ After them Zadok the son of Immer made repairs in front of his own house. After him Shemaiah the son of Shechaniah, the keeper of the East Gate, made repairs. ³⁰ After him Hananiah the son of Shelemiah, and Hanun, the sixth son of Zalaph, repaired another section. After him Meshullam the son of Berechiah made repairs in front of his dwelling. ³¹ After him Malchijah, one of the goldsmiths, made repairs as far as the house of the Nethinim and of the merchants, in front of the Miphkad Gate, and as far as the upper room at the corner. ³² And between the upper room at the corner, as far as the Sheep Gate, the goldsmiths and the merchants made repairs.

THE WALL DEFENDED AGAINST ENEMIES

4 But it so happened, when Sanballat heard that we were rebuilding the wall, that he was furious and very indignant, and mocked the Jews. ² And he spoke before his brethren and the army of Samaria, and said, "What are these feeble Jews doing? Will

they fortify themselves? Will they offer sacrifices? Will they complete it in a day? Will they revive the stones from the heaps of rubbish—stones that are burned?"

³ Now Tobiah the Ammonite was beside him, and he said, "Whatever they build, if even a fox goes up on it, he will break down their stone wall."

⁴ Hear, O our God, for we are despised; turn their reproach on their own heads, and give them as plunder to a land of captivity! ⁵ Do not cover their iniquity, and do not let their sin be blotted out from before You; for they have provoked You to anger before the builders.

⁶ So we built the wall, and the entire wall was joined together up to half its height, for the people had a mind to work.

⁷ Now it happened, when Sanballat, Tobiah, the Arabs, the Ammonites, and the Ashdodites heard that the walls of Jerusalem were being restored and the gaps were beginning to be closed, that they became very angry, ⁸ and all of them conspired together to come and attack Jerusalem and create confusion. ⁹ Nevertheless we made our prayer to our God, and because of them we set a watch against them day and night.

¹⁰ Then Judah said, "The strength of the laborers is failing, and there is so much rubbish that we are not able to build the wall."

¹¹ And our adversaries said, "They will neither know nor see anything, till we come into their midst and kill them and cause the work to cease."

¹² So it was, when the Jews who dwelt near them came, that they told us ten times, "From whatever place you turn, they will be upon us."

¹³ Therefore I positioned men behind the lower parts of the wall, at the openings; and I set the people according to their families, with their swords, their spears, and their bows. ¹⁴ And I looked, and arose and said to the nobles, to the leaders, and to the rest of the people, "Do not be afraid of them. Remember the Lord, great and awesome, and fight

for your brethren, your sons, your daughters, your wives, and your houses."

¹⁵ And it happened, when our enemies heard that it was known to us, and that God had brought their plot to nothing, that all of us returned to the wall, everyone to his work. ¹⁶ So it was, from that time on, that half of my servants worked at construction, while the other half held the spears, the shields, the bows, and wore armor; and the leaders were behind all the house of Judah. ¹⁷ Those who built on the wall, and those who carried burdens, loaded themselves so that with one hand they worked at construction, and with the other held a weapon. ¹⁸ Every one of the builders had his sword girded at his side as he built. And the one who sounded the trumpet was beside me.

¹⁹ Then I said to the nobles, the rulers, and the rest of the people, "The work is great and extensive, and we are separated far from one another on the wall. ²⁰ Wherever you hear the sound of the trumpet, rally to us there. Our God will fight for us."

²¹ So we labored in the work, and half of the men held the spears from daybreak until the stars appeared. ²² At the same time I also said to the people, "Let each man and his servant stay at night in Jerusalem, that they may be our guard by night and a working party by day." ²³ So neither I, my brethren, my servants, nor the men of the guard who followed me took off our clothes, except that everyone took them off for washing.

NEHEMIAH DEALS WITH OPPRESSION

5 And there was a great outcry of the people and their wives against their Jewish brethren. ² For there were those who said, "We, our sons, and our daughters are many; therefore let us get grain, that we may eat and live."

³ There were also some who said, "We have mortgaged our lands and vineyards and houses, that we might buy grain because of the famine."

⁴ There were also those who said, "We have borrowed money for the king's tax on our lands and vineyards. ⁵ Yet now our flesh is as the flesh of our brethren, our children as their children; and indeed we are forcing our sons and our daughters to be slaves, and some of our daughters have been brought into slavery. It is not in our power to redeem them, for other men have our lands and vineyards."

⁶ And I became very angry when I heard their outcry and these words. ⁷ After serious thought, I rebuked the nobles and rulers, and said to them, "Each of you is exacting usury from his brother." So I called a great assembly against them. ⁸ And I said to them, "According to our ability we have redeemed our Jewish brethren who were sold to the nations. Now indeed, will you even sell your brethren? Or should they be sold to us?"

Then they were silenced and found nothing to say. ⁹ Then I said, "What you are doing is not good. Should you not walk in the fear of our God because of the reproach of the nations, our enemies? ¹⁰ I also, with my brethren and my servants, am lending them money and grain. Please, let us stop this usury! ¹¹ Restore now to them, even this day, their lands, their vineyards, their olive groves, and their houses, also a hundredth of the money and the grain, the new wine and the oil, that you have charged them."

¹² So they said, "We will restore it, and will require nothing from them; we will do as you say."

Then I called the priests, and required an oath from them that they would do according to this promise. ¹³ Then I shook out the fold of my garment and said, "So may God shake out each man from his house, and from his property, who does not perform this promise. Even thus may he be shaken out and emptied."

And all the assembly said, "Amen!" and praised the Lord. Then the people did according to this promise.

THE GENEROSITY OF NEHEMIAH

¹⁴ Moreover, from the time that I was appointed to be their governor in the land of Judah, from the twentieth year until the thirty-second year of King Artaxerxes, twelve years, neither I nor my brothers ate the governor's provisions. ¹⁵ But the former governors who were before me laid burdens on the people, and took from them bread and wine, besides forty shekels of silver. Yes, even their servants bore rule over the people, but I did not do so, because of the fear of God. ¹⁶ Indeed, I also continued the work on this wall, and we did not buy any land. All my servants were gathered there for the work.

¹⁷ And at my table were one hundred and fifty Jews and rulers, besides those who came to us from the nations around us. ¹⁸ Now that which was prepared daily was one ox and six choice sheep. Also fowl were prepared for me, and once every ten days an abundance of all kinds of wine. Yet in spite of this I did not demand the governor's provisions, because the bondage was heavy on this people.

¹⁹ Remember me, my God, for good, according to all that I have done for this people.

CONSPIRACY AGAINST NEHEMIAH

6 Now it happened when Sanballat, Tobiah, Geshem the Arab, and the rest of our enemies heard that I had rebuilt the wall, and that there were no breaks left in it (though at that time I had not hung the doors in the gates), ² that Sanballat and Geshem sent to me, saying, "Come, let us meet together among the villages in the plain of Ono." But they thought to do me harm.

³ So I sent messengers to them, saying, "I am doing a great work, so that I cannot come down. Why should the work cease while I leave it and go down to you?"

⁴ But they sent me this message four times, and I answered them in the same manner.

⁵ Then Sanballat sent his

servant to me as before, the fifth time, with an open letter in his hand. ⁶ In it was written:

> It is reported among the nations, and Geshem says, that you and the Jews plan to rebel; therefore, according to these rumors, you are rebuilding the wall, that you may be their king. ⁷ And you have also appointed prophets to proclaim concerning you at Jerusalem, saying, "There is a king in Judah!" Now these matters will be reported to the king. So come, therefore, and let us consult together.

⁸ Then I sent to him, saying, "No such things as you say are being done, but you invent them in your own heart."

⁹ For they all were trying to make us afraid, saying, "Their hands will be weakened in the work, and it will not be done."

Now therefore, O God, strengthen my hands.

¹⁰ Afterward I came to the house of Shemaiah the son of Delaiah, the son of Mehetabel, who was a secret informer; and he said, "Let us meet together in the house of God, within the temple, and let us close the doors of the temple, for they are coming to kill you; indeed, at night they will come to kill you."

¹¹ And I said, "Should such a man as I flee? And who is there such as I who would go into the temple to save his life? I will not go in!" ¹² Then I perceived that God had not sent him at all, but that he pronounced this prophecy against me because Tobiah and Sanballat had hired him. ¹³ For this reason he was hired, that I should be afraid and act that way and sin, so that they might have cause for an evil report, that they might reproach me.

¹⁴ My God, remember Tobiah and Sanballat, according to these their works, and the prophetess Noadiah and the rest of the prophets who would have made me afraid.

THE WALL COMPLETED

¹⁵ So the wall was finished on the twenty-fifth day of Elul, in fifty-two days. ¹⁶ And it happened, when all our enemies heard of it, and all the nations around us saw these things, that they were very disheartened in their own eyes; for they perceived that this work was done by our God.

¹⁷ Also in those days the nobles of Judah sent many letters to Tobiah, and the letters of Tobiah came to them. ¹⁸ For many in Judah were pledged to him, because he was the son-in-law of Shechaniah the son of Arah, and his son Jehohanan had married the daughter of Meshullam the son of Berechiah. ¹⁹ Also they reported his good deeds before me, and reported my words to him. Tobiah sent letters to frighten me.

Mission:Dignity

*A*ll of the author's royalties and any proceeds from *The James Code*, *The Jesus Code*, *The Joshua Code*, *The Daniel Code*, *The Believer's Code*, *The Christmas Code*, and now *The Nehemiah Code* go to the support of Mission:Dignity, a ministry of the Dallas-based GuideStone Financial Resources that enables thousands of retired ministers (and, in most cases, their widows) who are living near the poverty level to live out their days with dignity and security. Many of them spent their pastoral ministry in small churches that were unable to provide adequately for their retirement. They also lived in church-owned parsonages and, upon their vocational retirement, had to vacate them as well. Mission:Dignity is a way of letting these good and godly servants know they are not forgotten and will be cared for in their declining years.

All of the expenses of this ministry are paid out of an endowment that has been raised for such, so everyone who gives to Mission:Dignity can be assured that every cent of their gift goes to one of these precious saints in need.

For additional information regarding this ministry, please go to www.guidestone.org and click on the Mission:Dignity icon, or call toll-free at 1-888-98-GUIDE (1-888-984-8433).

ABOUT THE AUTHOR

*F*or more than twenty-five years, O. S. Hawkins served pastorates, including the First Baptist Church in Fort Lauderdale, Florida, and the First Baptist Church in Dallas, Texas. A native of Fort Worth, he has three earned degrees (BBA, MDiv, and DMin) as well as several honorary degrees. He is president of GuideStone Financial Resources, which serves 250,000 pastors, church staff members, missionaries, doctors, nurses, university professors, and other workers in various Christian organizations with their retirement and benefit service needs. He is the author of more than thirty books, including *The Joshua Code*, *The Jesus Code*, *The James Code*, *The Daniel Code*, *The Believer's Code*, *The Christmas Code*, and *The Nehemiah Code*, and he preaches regularly at conferences, universities, business groups, and churches across the nation. He and his wife, Susie, have two married daughters and six grandchildren.

Follow O. S. Hawkins on Twitter @OSHawkins.
Visit www.oshawkins.com for free resources.

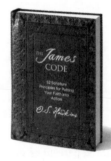

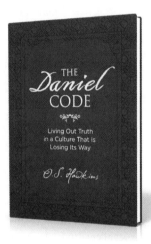